IMMERSED

God's Desire For Our Lives

James T. Martin

Lowgap Publishers
167 Shady Grove Church Rd.
Winston-Salem, NC 27107
1999

Immersed, God's Desire for Our Lives
By James T. Martin
Copyrighted 1996

All scripture references were taken from the Holy Bible, New International Version.

For more information about the author, to order more books, or to receive the leader's guide for small group use of *Immersed* visit our **web site**: www.shadygroveumc.com
E-mail address: lowgapper@yahoo.com

Published by:

Lowgap Publishers
167 Shady Grove Church Rd.
Winston-Salem, NC 27107

ISBN: 0-7392-0175-1
Second Printing

Printed in the United States by:
Morris Publishing
3212 East Highway 30
Kearney, NE 68847
1-800-650-7888

**Dedicated to my Parents:
Dr. O.Dean and Rev. Sandra Martin**

When God first started showing me the truths contained in this book, those truths were already familiar due to my parent's loving and faithful witness.

Table Of Contents

CHAPTER	TITLE	PAGE
Chapter 1	Getting the Picture Straight	3
Chapter 2	Fill My Cup Lord	8
Chapter 3	And You Will Receive Power	18
Chapter 4	Unlocking The Door	26
Chapter 5	Finding Value	39
Chapter 6	The Music is never heard unless....	51
Chapter 7	Breaking The Elevator Syndrome	58
Chapter 8	So That The World Will Be...	68
Chapter 9	Blessed Assurance	73
Chapter 10	Looking through Clearer Glass	77
Chapter 11	Following The Hash Marks...	84
Chapter 12	Leaving The Wine Press	93
Chapter 13	A Calm in The Storm	104
Chapter 14	A Reason To Smile	112
Section II	Getting Over The Wall	124
Chapter 15	The Lure of Safe Religion	128
Chapter 16	Declarations of Faith or Mantras	134
Chapter 17	Loosing Control	145
Chapter 18	We're Not Convinced	150
Chapter 19	It Costs Too Much	155
Chapter 20	It's Not Possible	159
Section III	Now What?	167
Chapter 21	Know The Truth	169
Chapter 22	Set Sail	176
Chapter 23	Keep Looking Ahead	186
Chapter 24	The Gift or The Giver	190
Chapter 25	You Can't Fly With Eagles If...	197
Chapter 26	Scraping The Pot	203
Chapter 27	Break	209
Chapter 28	Say Please	223
Chapter 29	Listen For The Tick	232
Chapter 30	Take The Step	239

<u>FORWARD</u>

I can't tell you how much trouble I have had getting the first few pages of this book down. I must have rewritten this section at least a hundred times. I guess what I've been looking for was something eye catching and dramatic that would say to you, the reader, "This is a great book. I'm really looking forward to what God is going to say to me through this book."

But nothing has felt right up to this point..... except what I'm about to write now. Here goes:

"This is really a great book. What you have in your hands is my sit down talk with you about what God has been showing me from His Word and for *our* lives. The book was written because God wouldn't leave me alone until I wrote it. The focus of the book is holiness. I know for some that is a somewhat scary word. In fact, when I first started submitting this work for publication, most of the companies encouraged me to avoid using that word altogether due to the fact that it carries a great deal of baggage with it. So, if you don't like "holiness," then use "righteousness," or "full surrender." Whatever makes you happy. The basic gist is that God wants all of us so that He can fill us with all of Himself. *That's* holiness.

Sit back, relax, and pretend we're having a conversation. Feel free to laugh every once in awhile. It's good for you. Write in the margins (if it's your book). Copy a phrase or two and keep it eternally alive through forwarded e-mail. Enjoy. Let God speak to you through these words. He has definitely been speaking to me.

God has a great design and desire for our lives. He wants us to be *immersed*.

Immersed

God's Desire for Our Lives

CHAPTER 1
Getting the Picture

"Be holy even as your father in heaven is holy." (Matthew 5:48)

A few years ago I was leading a youth discussion group when one of the young ladies in the group asked, "What does it mean to be holy?".

Though that topic does not come up frequently in daily conversation, it was not the first time I had ever been asked that question. It was the first time, however, that I was literally given a picture ("Vision," if that makes it sound more spiritual) which helped give me a clearer understanding of what God means by the word "holy." And in that instance, with that picture, this book was born.

While the picta-"vision" was fresh and running through my head, I quickly picked up a piece of paper and a pen and started scribbling out what I was being given. I was not aware of the fact that the rest of the group was having their own little discussion about holiness and didn't care in the least that I was off somewhere else in the process of having my life turned around. Finally, after I had written down most of what God had allowed me to see, I looked up and said, "Alright, here's the answer."

The awkward silence that followed from the rest of the group was due to the fact that by the time I had finished writing everything down, they had already left the question of holiness and were dealing with something totally unrelated. One of them asked, "What answer?"

"The answer to, "What does it mean to be holy?"" I answered.

"We already covered that," one of them said.

"Humor me," I responded. "I want us to go over it again."

The following is an abbreviated version of the conversation.

I started with the old Campus Life picture, drew a circle, and said, "Here is your life. God created you, and you were perfect." The circle drawn was pure and clean. I then drew a seat in the middle and said, "Here is the throne of your life. The one who calls the shots, makes the decisions, and leads the way, sits on this throne. **YOU** are the person seated on the throne *before* any commitment to Jesus is made."

I then proceeded to awe and inspire them with a proportionally correct stick figure placed on the throne.

"The problem is," I continued, "when we are left to our own choices, we naturally choose self-centered and self-serving ways. Because of this, we make self-centered and self-serving choices which mess up the picture and dirty what God created perfect."

Awing them again with my artistic abilities, garbage was drawn around the inside of the circle.

So as not to lose anyone in the translation, I have provided below a close approximation to what had been drawn up to that point.

After everyone stopped rolling on the floor from uncontrollable laughter, I finished my illustration.   "Before

Christ, our lives are filled with garbage, sin, guilt, greed.... you name it, it's in there. When you give your life to Christ, you are first of all washed clean and made new."

I quoted Psalms 51:7, "Touch me with hyssop and I will be clean. Wash me and I will be whiter than snow." I then added, "*this* is what Christ does for us because of his death on the cross."

I then erased the dirt and smudges from the middle of the circle.

"But, when we give our lives to Christ, we are not only receiving forgiveness from our past, we are also being made new.   As new creations we are open for Jesus to set up residence in our hearts, to have a living relationship with us, and to become Lord of our lives. Now, if Christ truly is Lord of our lives, if He is the one who calls the shots, makes the decisions, and leads the way, where should He sit?"

"On the throne!" they responded with guarded enthusiasm.

"Right!" I said trying to restrain my excitement.

"Who would sit on the throne of a 'born again' life?" I asked again.

"Jesus would," they intoned once more.

With that, I erased my stick figure and placed a cross on the throne.

"This artistically magnificent picture," I continued, "is what most of you call 'getting saved' or 'being born again.' Your past is forgiven and your hearts are cleaned up because of what Jesus did *for* you on the cross and *in* you when you received His forgiveness. But don't stop there! That's the problem. Too many well meaning Christians think that this is all God has in mind for us. The truth is that God wants to make us holy;...... pure."

I then asked, "If God's ultimate desire for us is to be holy, to be completely His, what would that look like in this diagram? Where would *you* be in the picture? If salvation is cleaning up the picture and allowing Christ to sit on the thrown, what does it look like to be made holy? Where should I put your stick figure?"

Before you continue reading, take a moment to answer this question yourself.

WHERE SHOULD *YOUR* STICK FIGURE BE?

Are you finished?   Good.   Here are a few of the responses I received from my small group.

One young man said, "Kneeling at Jesus' feet."

I like that! If there is anything we are quickly losing in Christianity today, it is the concept of God being worthy of our falling before Him in adoration, praise, and worship.

Another young lady said, "Standing behind Jesus one hundred percent."

That image goes along with the song "Where He leads me, I will follow. I'll go with Him, with Him, all the way." She apparently had a good grasp of Jesus as Lord.

Among the other two or three responses that followed, the one I liked best was when a young girl said, "Sitting on Jesus' lap."

That image received a number of, "Yeah"s and a "Hey! That's good!" from the rest of the group.   After a little discussion I discovered they liked that image best because it gave them a sense of God being close by with themselves held tightly in His peaceful, loving arms.

Though their answers were good, I had to break the news to them that they had not given me the million dollar answer I was looking for.

THE Picture

By this time they were all getting a little agitated and were anxiously waiting for me to share my earth shattering revelation. I paused for just the right amount of dramatic effect and said, "Holiness is not about our bowing before, standing behind, or sitting on God's lap. Holiness is *God's* Spirit filling *our* mind, life, and soul to the point that ***we are no longer in the picture.***"

Go back and read that last sentence again. *That* is *the* cornerstone of this book. Not only is it the cornerstone of this book, but I have found it to clearly be the cornerstone of *The Book* -God's Word. "Getting out of the picture" is not another interesting religious topic to experiment with when you don't have anything better to do. I am totally convinced that this is God's clear goal for every person who turns to Him. Read it! Pray about it! Allow God's Spirit to speak to you through it.

I'll repeat it just to make sure you get it: **"Holiness, God's ultimate desire for us, is that we become so filled with God's Holy Spirit that what others see is not us, but *God* in us. We are no longer in the picture."**

The rest of this book is an attempt to express this truth; to describe the unbelievable joy I have experienced as I have begun to discover that truth; to show the power that awaits everyone who begins to experience that truth, and to move in the direction of God's ultimate goal for our lives, i.e. to be out of the picture.

CHAPTER 2
Fill My Cup Lord

"Then he (Jesus) said to them all, 'If any want to become my followers, let them deny themselves and take up their cross daily and follow me. For those who want to save their life will lose it, and those who lose their life for my sake will save it.'" *(Luke 9:23 & 24 NIV)*

Here again is the statement made to those youth in my small group: "We are not to stand behind Jesus, sit on His lap, or kneel before Him. God's design is that we are out of the picture."

If you want to cut to the chase and avoid reading the rest of the book, in a nutshell this is what the statement is saying: ***God wants us fully, totally, and completely surrendered to Him and filled with His Spirit. God wants every aspect of the old self to be sacrificed, and His love, power, presence, and Spirit to take its place. God's desire for all of His children is that, as others look at us, they will see His Spirit. To paraphrase John The Baptist: "The Spirit of Christ must increase and I must decrease" (John 3:30).***

Obviously, this statement goes **way beyond** what most people think of when they think of "getting saved" or being "born again". In fact, one of the real motivations for writing this book is to help others get beyond a very shallow concept of "Salvation" and discover what it truly means to belong *to*, and be in a relationship *with*, God.

One of the hardest nuts to crack in helping someone begin to understand a relationship with God is that many people see the *beginning* of that relationship (getting saved) as the *end* instead of simply the first step of a life long journey.

For the record, our salvation experience is not the end of the journey. It is just the beginning! Think of it this way.

8

When a couple getting married says, "I do," they are officially "hitched." They are finished getting married, but they have only taken the first step toward having a marriage. In the same way, God's desire and design for us is that we not only take the first step in a relationship with Him and have our *past* forgiven through the sacrifice of Christ, but that we make our *futures* available to the Spirit of Christ. This is a life long process.

Paul had the right idea when he said,

> "Not that I have already obtained all this, or have already been made perfect, but I press on to take hold of that for which Christ Jesus took hold of me. Brothers, I do not consider myself yet to have taken hold of it. But one thing I do: Forgetting what is behind and straining toward what is ahead, I press on toward the goal to win the prize for which God has called me heavenward in Christ Jesus." (Phillipians 4:12-14 NIV)

To Paul, God's goal in Christ was not *just* to forgive the world of its sin. God's goal wasn't even *just* to enable humanity to come into God's presence. God's ultimate goal was to create a holy priesthood, cleaned up by the Sacrifice of Christ, given new life through His resurrection, and then *filled* with His Spirit. It was the "filled with His Spirit" part that Paul recognized and "pressed on" toward.

One of Paul's marvelous gifts was that he understood what Jesus meant when He said, "If anyone wants to become my follower, let him deny himself and take up his cross daily and follow me. For whoever wants to save his life *will lose it*, and whoever *loses his life* for my sake will save it." (Luke 9:23-24 NIV) To use the picture I was given: God's goal is that we are so fully surrendered that we are ultimately **out of the picture**!

"But," you might be thinking, "Isn't 'out of the picture' a bit strong?"

Think of it this way. Jesus did not say, "If you want to follow me, just surrender whatever isn't too inconvenient for you and still allows you to call the shots." He said, "Whoever would *lose* his life!" He did not say, "I want to give you life, so let me *borrow it* from you for awhile. I'll give it back. I promise." He said in essence, "If you want to find life, real life, then the old one has to go. *You* have to die in order to live." That may sound harsh, but it makes perfect sense.

Have you ever been walking along a road and found an old mug laying in a ditch? If you have, most likely you didn't pluck it out of the mud and muck, dip it a nearby creek, and take a drink. If you did, I will be sure to bring my own glassware when I come to visit. Once you pluck the mug out of the mire, what *would* you do with the dirty, gunked up, slimy, bug infested, full of leaves mug from the ditch? For arguments sake, just go along with the analogy and agree that you would pick it up and take it home. Now what? Most of us would clean up the outside in order to see exactly what we had. The more you clean, the better it looks. The better it looks, the more excited you become about having it.

What now? The *outside* is clean. From most people's perspective the mug is ready to use. Is it? Not unless you like a little gunked up, slimy, bug infested muck with your orange juice. Would you be satisfied with a clean exterior and, regardless of the conditions of the interior, pour the orange juice in the mug and take a drink? I would hope not! Why not? First of all, with all the old garbage still clinging to the sides, there probably is rnot a lot of room in the mug for the orange juice. Secondly,..... it would taste bad. What would you do?

Read the next line carefully.

In order for you to use the mug and be able to *fill it up*, it's going to have to be *emptied* first! That is exactly what Jesus is saying. In order for something to be filled with anything new, whatever was present in the first place has to be removed.

Would you fry eggs in a pan, and then turn around and, without washing the pan, use it to boil water for hot chocolate? Of course not! Who wants hot chocolate-a-la-egg? If a pot is going to be used, it is thoroughly cleaned, inside and out, to make room for its next occupant *and* to avoid contamination. Clearly, throughout the Word, God's desire is that we are *emptied* so that we can be completely filled to overflowing with the Spirit of God..... with no other contaminants present.

But what about **"filled until we are out of the picture"**? Isn't that more pointed language than "lose one's life to save it"? Doesn't "out of the picture" go a little too far? Isn't the desired result to be completely filled to overflowing with the Spirit of God? That statement says quite a bit, "Completely filled" with the Spirit of God!" Is it necessary that we add, "until we are out of the picture?" According to the scriptures, YES! In order for us to be filled to overflowing with the Spirit of God there can't be anything else in the picture *but* the Spirit of God.

But, "You are out of the picture" sounds so..... un-American. It sounds like we become puppets on a string with absolutely no will or resolve of our own. "You are out of the picture" sounds like we cease to exist. The wording seems to fly in the face of Jesus' promise that we would find abundant life in him. How would we know that abundant life if we were no longer in the picture?

Have any of those questions been running through your mind? Are you having problems getting past the aspect of being out of the picture? If, because of some difficulties with this point, you are planning on using this book as a door stop in the garage, you might want to skip ahead to section two. That section addresses some of the problems we have with the concept of *complete* surrender, and attempts to help in the process of getting beyond the road blocks.

Please feel free to jump ahead and work through section two. Trust me, the book will not self-destruct if you do.

If you decided to stick around, in a nutshell, *the* reason I have been able to continue past my own road blocks about the issue of complete surrender is the simple fact I have discovered that the further I press on toward that goal, the

Spirit of God being the only presence in my picture, the more I realize it is precisely in total surrender that I find *life*! I will say it again for clarity's sake. The more aspects of my life that I am willing to give up; the larger I allow God's Spirit flame to grow and burn away the dross -the garbage- within me; the more of me that is filled with His Spirit, the more I become who I want to be; was intended to be, and most of all, enjoy being!

One of our real problems is we -especially Americans- like to convince ourselves that *we* are in control. But if the dim light of truth could make its way through the muck of misleading lies, we would have to admit that *we* are never really in control. Rather, we are always influenced by a force greater than ourselves. Whether that force be God or society, one or the other will influence our choices and direct our paths. The ironic part of this whole surrender issue is that when I was in control and God had limited, if any, visitation rights, it was *then* that I was the puppet on the string with little, if any, control of my own. The truth is that "*the world*" held the strings and called the shots, not me! When "they" said, "Not acceptable," I would change. When the establishment held out the golden carrot, I would jump. Like the dog in Pavlov's experiment, when the "world" rang the bell, I would salivate for whatever "they" said was my goal. It was when Jesus stepped in, that slowly *real* control started to return; real direction and purpose began to take shape. Now? Now my ship is guided through the reefs by The One who made the oceans. Now I march to the beat of The Master drummer. There is finally control in my life. Ultimately I guess we really do have some control. We ultimately control who gets to stand behind the wheel and steer the ship. Just don't make the mistake in thinking **you** ever will.

Maybe this analogy will help those who are having trouble getting beyond this whole "who's in control" issue. Let's say you are a wimpy little kid in second grade. Every day, the bully of the school threatens to beat you up if you don't give him your lunch money. Just to make sure you know he is serious, he pushes you around a little bit from time to time. More or less this kid controls the second grade. He has his own organized crime for extorting milk money and making people do stupid things for his personal pleasure. You, of course, *do* have a choice about whether to give him your money or do the ridiculous things he wants you to do. You have *some* degree of choice, but with the threat of great physical harm and complete social annihilation, you don't have *much* of a choice.

The day of salvation finally arrives! A kid five times this bully's size is transferred to your school. Low and behold, this big kid likes *you*. No! He doesn't just like you. He *loves* you. He wants to help you in any way he can. You know what you want. You want to get out from under the controlling hand of the school bully. Finally, the long awaited day arrives. It's the face off! Your friend,.... "Jesus," stands toe to toe with the bully. What would you do? Would you jump in front of Jesus and proclaim, "Now wait a minute. I don't want to lose my personhood. I'm an American you know! I must maintain the facade of self-reliance even if it means my total destruction. A man has to do what a man has to do. Thanks for the offer, but I'll handle this on my own?"

I don't think so, although some pride-filled idiot might. What would be the result if you did? Instant death! The bully would tear you limb from limb because of your having a part in his embarrassment. Would anyone be impressed at your gallant stand and self sufficiency? The undertaker probably would. If he wasn't impressed, he would at least appreciate the business!

Think about it. If you were the little kid on the play ground, and some huge, muscle bound guy wanted to fight for you, what would you do? I would *LET HIM*!! Not only would I let him, I would stand back and cheer him on. Not only would I cheer him on, I would take great pleasure in the defeat of my enemy. Why? Because that enemy who cared nothing *for* me, had control *over* me. With Jesus as my new companion, I can go into the lunch room any time I want. I can walk the halls safely. I can take a few extra curricular activities because I don't have to worry about getting mugged on the way home. WOW! I have real freedom! I can *now* begin to become the person I was always intended to be.

Get the point!

The more I allow the big kid, Jesus, to fight my battles, the more I find freedom, joy, celebration and LIFE . Am I ashamed? Not on your life! Not once I realized the alternative was a bloody nose.

Jesus said, "Whoever wants to save his life must *lose it*."

One of the frustrating things about trying to communicate truths of faith is dthere are no perfect parallels. Every analogy and illustration may communicate some aspects of the truth, but there is never an analogy which can communicate all of them. I know what God has graciously helped me to begin experiencing. The problem is trying to adequately explain and universally communicate something which has NO common analogy.

The image of "Total Surrender" is close, but it still has the feel of God standing apart from me.

Jesus' words "lose your life" are closer, but they carry with them such negative overtones for our modern day "ME" society that most people never get beyond the "lose" portion to the "find your life" part.

The wimpy second grader with the big friend falls way short because what I'm trying to communicate is more of an internal change with resulting external differences.

Even the cleansed and scraped pot falls short if for no other reason than it doesn't feel like it completely clarifies what I know to be the truth.

I guess if there were a perfect analogy, there would not be as many books around attempting to explain it. I could simply write, "Think of a ....", send it to my publisher, have 1,000,000 copies printed, and go fishing.

Though I can not give you a *complete* parallel of what God has in store for us, I can give you the word which has been pounding in my mind since I began the real heart-wrenching work of writing this book: **"Immersed"**.

"Immersed"..... God desires desperately that every pore of me is permeated with every ounce of Him. The glorious life God has offered us is like a sponge immersed in water. We would be so filled with The Spirit of God that when we are "squeezed" by the world, all that comes out is God.

To get a good feel of *this* particular analogy, go find a large bowl and a dry, used sponge. If the sponge isn't dried and rock hard, then find one that is dried to the core. Now, fill the bowl with water. The water represents the presence and Spirit of God. Put just a tip of the sponge in the water. What happens? The tip of the sponge soaks up the water like a thirsty man stranded in the desert. If you were to set the sponge aside, how long do you think it would take to dry up? One hour? Two? It really depends on where you set it and the conditions around it. If you set the sponge in direct sunlight on a 95 degree day, that little tip will be dried out in a matter of minutes.

That little tip is the majority of "church goers" in America today. No real commitment. No real connection with the presence of God. They dip just enough of their lives into God's presence to wet their lips and then move on. The silly part is they move on and then wonder why God seems so far away. HELLO!

Now take the sponge and plunge it down completely into the bowl of water and then take it out immediately. What happens? If you have normal water and the type of sponge I described, most, and possibly all of the sponge, became saturated with the water -the presence and Spirit of God. That plunging is a salvation experience in Jesus Christ. It's wonderful, moving, cleansing, refreshing,.... wet! When a person comes out of a real experience in Jesus, he or she is just dripping Christ all over the place.

Now place the sponge out in the sun. What happens? Again, it depends on the conditions. The hotter and more harsh the conditions, and the longer the sponge is out of the water, the faster it dries up. Sadly, *that* single plunge is exactly what most Christians believe Christianity is all about: A one time plunge into lake Jesus. Consequently, "dried up" is precisely what most Christians become because, thinking they've completed the one time transaction, they jump out and then wallow around on the sand until the harsh conditions around them have dried up every sign of life that was there.

Now take the sponge and put it in the bowl of water and leave it there. Pull it out and squeeze it. What happens? The Spirit of God oozes out. Put the sponge back in and then pull it out again. Same thing? Yep. Now stick it back in and leave it!!

Immersed!

Is that the perfect analogy? Not yet. It *would be* perfect if you could find a sponge that dissolved in water and then put the bowl over a spring that would never run dry. If you could meet those conditions, you would have, I believe, the perfect picture of what God has in store for us. No part of us would be getting in God's way in our lives. When someone looked at us, they would see only the Spirit of God..... and the Spirit would just keep on flowing. Jesus said it, "Whoever drinks the water I give him will never thirst. Indeed, the water I give him will become in him a spring of water welling up to eternal life." (John 4:14 NIV)

Just think of what *could be* in our lives. So often the focus of spiritual and religious teaching is: What can I get God to do *for me*. That teaching is not only unbiblical, but it is one of the anchors which keeps the Christian faith stranded in the shallows and never pushing out into the deep water God wants us to sail in. The essence of being immersed in God's Spirit.... of "getting out of the picture," is what can God do *in* me and *through* me by *filling* me. *That* is the destination of our journey!

What does that destination look like?

Theoretically we might be starting to get a grasp on God's desire for us, but what exactly does it mean in the real, "rubber meets the road" part of life?

What are the benefits; the life-giving realities; the magnificent beauty of being fully immersed in the Spirit of God? What happens? How would it affect my daily life? How would I feel?

Read on. The following chapters contain just the tip of the iceberg of that which I am discovering to be the truth in my own life as I *begin* the process of getting out of the picture...... of being immersed in the Spirit of God.... of making my way toward the destination to which God is calling all of us.

CHAPTER 3

And You Will Receive Power!

"While staying with them, he ordered them not to leave Jerusalem, but to wait there for the promise of the Father. 'This,' he said, 'is what you have heard from me; for John baptized with water, but you will be baptized with the Holy Spirit not many days from now.'......'But you will receive power when the Holy Spirit has come upon you.."
(Acts 1:3,5,8 NIV)

A number of years ago I was strongly encouraged by my District Superintendent to attend a planned "minister's week." The instructor for the week was the type of "minister" who tended to be more caught up in theory than in literal and practical application.   In other words, he liked to talk intellectually about everything but *do* nothing.

During the weekend our instructor shared with us a personal story about a summer during his college years when he served as an intern for a United Methodist mission group in a Caribbean Island chain. He said that for most of the summer the mission's emphasis was being met. Because of the financial backing and the experienced help, the mission was able to feed the hungry, clothe the naked, reach out to lonely people, and lead the local people in worship services. I noticed that as long as the instructor was talking about this aspect of the mission's ministry, he had a smile on his face, and seemed to be reliving some pleasant memories.

His countenance soon changed, however. A frown stretched across his face, his eyes closed in a slight squint and he said, with flaring nostrils, "However, there was one.... charismatic there who got carried away. This young man had energy and a magnetic personality. Because of his magnetism, people were drawn to him and to what he said.   This

18

charismatic believed the United Methodist Church on the island was lagging behind in its witnessing for Jesus." The instructor hissed out the word "witnessing". "Because this person believed the mission was not fulfilling its ministry," the instructor continued, "this young preacher went off and started worship services outside of the scheduled mission's program."

To make a very long story semi-short, according to our instructor a large number of people came to hear this young preacher. He pointed out that "supposedly" many of these people who came were lead to Christ. But then a problem arose when they wanted to be baptized. Since these people had come to know the Lord through this young preacher, they wanted *him* to take part in the baptism. The young preacher went to the governing body of Methodism on that island and excitedly told them about this wonderful opportunity. There were, however, two problems according to the governing body. First of all, the preacher was not ordained and so could not do the baptism without presiding elders present. Secondly, the people wanted the baptism to be done in a river, but the governing body said that they would only do it on Sunday and inside the church. So, contrary to the presiding elder's wishes, and because of the people's strong desire to be baptized in the river, the young minister held a service of baptism one Saturday on the river without the Elders of his church present. About this point, our instructor paused. I think it was for dramatic effect. Then he asked, "Were the actions of that young preacher right or wrong?"

I can now say that I have actually seen someone's jaw drop to the ground and their eyes bug out of their head. When the instructor asked that question -obviously expecting a response from us in the negative- the vast majority of the minister's present said, "If the governing body was more interested in religious ritual than in personal commitment to Christ, then what the young preacher did was right."

After the instructor picked his jaw up off the floor and put his eye-balls back in their sockets, he launched into a long dissertation about church ritual and the sanctity of baptism. Finally, he ended with this statement, "Well, regardless of what you think, that minister *did* start a movement. It had a big impact; many people were *supposedly* -that word again- "saved," and more were baptized. But after a number of years, the movement fizzled out." Then he leaned forward with an "I told you so" look on his face and said, "And the Methodist church is still there."

A friend of mine was sitting next to me when the instructor said that. My friend leaned over and whispered in my ear, "I know about that island. That movement probably did more good for the Kingdom of God than the Methodist church has done in 100 years."

When he sat back in his seat, these words of John Wesley immediately popped into my head, "I do not fear that the people called Methodist will cease to exist on the face of Europe or America. But I do fear lest they exist as a dead sect, having the form of religion and **no power**."

Did you catch the end of that quote? Wesley said, "But I do fear lest they exist as a dead sect, having the form of religion and *no power*." "No power!"

Sadly to say, in many ways Wesley's worst fears have come true. And "powerless" is not just applicable to the Methodist church alone. It applies to far too many of our churches and denominations, yet power is exactly what people are looking for.

It is the cry I constantly hear inside the church, outside the church, in the streets, in the Sunday School rooms, in hospital corridors, and from bar stools. People want to know where they can find *power*!

People look at the church with its padded pews, stained glass windows, and endless bickering and ask, "What are they doing to change the world?"

"Where is something that will make a difference in my life?"

The people in the pews stare blankly at the pulpit as the ministers lounge around rattling on for 30 minutes attempting to be theologically and politically correct, and ultimately doing nothing but offering up bland, reheated leftovers with little nourishment and even less excitement.

"Where's the power?!"

The non-Christian is asking, "Am I alone? What will have any *real* and *lasting* impact in my life?"

The Christians sitting in the pews, Bible studies, committee meetings, *and* pulpits are wondering why life has no meaning. They know they have had some type of salvation experience, yet there seems to be something missing. There is no power! Bishop Wilcke, in his book "And Are We Yet Alive", described what people see most often when they look at the church. He was referring to the United Methodist Church, but I believe it applies in many aspects to many mainline denominations today. He said:

"Once we were a Wesley revival, full of enthusiasm, fired by the Spirit, running the race set before us like a sprinter trying to win the prize. The world was our parish; we were determined to 'publish the glad tiding in the full light of the sun.' Our Wesley inspired dream and directive was to spread Scriptural holiness across the continent. Circuit riders raced over hill and valley. New churches were established in every hamlet. Our missionaries encircled the globe."

"Now we are tired, listless, fueled only by the nostalgia of former days, walking with a droop, eyes on the ground, discouraged, putting one foot ahead of the other like a tired old man who remembers, but can no longer perform." ("And Are We Yet Alive" By Bishop Richard Wilcke)

You can almost see the grimace on the souls of those who are trying to figure out why, after they have joined the church and done all the proper ritual, their lives are still so empty, lost, and alone. "I'm at the end of my rope," they say.

People want to know where the power is to *live*! People want to know where the power is to make a difference! Christians want to know where the power is that would enable them to stand boldly and proclaim the Gospel to a dying world.

The dying world is wanting to know why the Christians don't have the power to make a stand. Where is the power?

Jesus gave the answer: "For you will receive **power** when the Holy Spirit comes upon you,.."

What jumps up and waves its hand as the number one real, tangible result of a person getting out of the picture and immersing their life in the Spirit of God is the presence and outpouring of power!

"And you will receive power when the Holy Spirit comes upon you,..."

"Power!" "Ability." "Strength beyond myself." You pick the word. Whatever makes you happy. Whatever best communicates that *now* I can, when before I could not.

Please note that I am not talking about some manipulative tool to get my way by impressing and influencing people. Simon, in the eighth chapter of the book of Acts, thought the power of the Holy Spirit was something to be selfishly acquired. When he saw Peter and John doing great miracles, he had the nerve to offer them money to buy the power so that he could do the same tricks, earn a few bucks, and make a name for himself in the process. That is not the type of power I am talking about. I am talking about a power that takes us from "There's no way I can do this, Lord." to "When do I get started?!" It is a power which moves the sheepish church sitter off the pew and into the battle..... *for*, and on behalf of, the Kingdom of God!

Think of Peter at Pentecost (Acts chapter 2). Not only did being filled with the Holy Spirit enable him to move out past the locked door of fear, but the Spirit gave him the power to speak boldly in the name of Christ. Before Peter's Pentecost experience, he was always putting his foot in his mouth and speaking before he thought. Peter never had a problem speaking his mind. The fact that he stood up that day and addressed the huge crowd was not all that miraculous. The old Peter probably would have relished the attention. The miracle was that when he spoke, lives where changed, and souls were saved. Why? Because Peter was a willing vessel for the Spirit to use and send power *through*.

"And you will receive power when the Holy Spirit comes on you,...."

Since the start of this chapter, I have been trying to come up with one major example of the power of the Spirit moving and working in *my* life. The problem has not been trying to think of examples, but narrowing it down to just *one*. Without any shallow humility implied, I can honestly say that every time I stand to speak for Jesus Christ, I can do so *only* as I am able to get out of the picture and allow the power of God's Spirit to fill me. But with all those other examples aside, I guess the best example of God giving me the power to speak would be the day of my father's memorial service.

My mother asked if I would like to say something at my father's funeral. Because I wanted to make sure some specific things were said, I told her, "Yes." We waited four days to hold the service in order to allow family and friends to arrive from out of town. That gave me plenty of time to think and pray about what to say.

Finally, the day came, and I started to feel just the slightest bit nervous. It was when I walked into the church with my family that what I was about to do sank in. There were at least 1800 people in attendance, along with most of the District Superintendents of the Florida Annual Conference and a few Bishops thrown in for good measure. This was easily going to be the largest and most intimidating crowd I had ever spoken to. In fact, it is still the largest group of people I have had the privilege of addressing. But it really was not the number, or the dignitaries which were so intimidating. What was making me sick to my stomach was the fact that I was not going to speak about my father as much as deal with where the Gospel fits into the whole set of messy questions about healing, miracles, death, and all of those "easy to explain subjects."

A little sarcasm is implied with that last statement.

I still remember sitting with my family, about the third pew back in the middle section of the church. I was doing my best to listen to what others were saying and to the beautiful songs the choir was singing. I was doing my best, but to no avail. All I could hear in my head was, "What have you gotten yourself into now you idiot?! You're barely going to be able to stand up there without crying. How do you think you can help these people when you're not sure of what you believe yourself?!"

I was about to tell my wife I was having a stroke and that she needed to take me home, when I closed my eyes and said in desperation, "Lord, what am I going to do?!" At that moment, everything became deathly quiet. I knew where I was, but I could not hear a thing. I still had my eyes closed, when I felt a presence and an urging say, "Rest. I am with you. Rest."

After a few minutes I opened my eyes and discovered that I had been sitting there for a number of minutes with a silly grin on my face. Was I still anxious? You bet! But not the "anxious" you are thinking about. I was anxious to get up there! In the quiet, I had been reminded that this was not an event to show off Jim Martin or to uplift his wonderful dad. I was in that situation to exalt the Lord, and if I would step out of the way a little, HE, God, would give me the words to do it. In other words, I was off the hook. I had the freedom simply to stand, open my mouth, and trust in the One who said, "I am with you always." (Matthew 28:20)

I didn't just take part in the service, I was the one who closed it. I really do not remember much of what I said. I had to go back a few months later and watch the video just to remember. I still marvel at literally the hundreds of people who came up to me after the service and told me that what I said had helped *them* handle the situation. I knew better. I had said nothing. I had accomplished nothing. I had simply made myself available to God's Spirit and was given what was needed at the time to accomplish His work; **POWER**.

If I am left to my own abilities, I fall. Regardless of what the "self-help" bunch have to say, I fall. BUT! as I move out of the picture, and the presence of the God of the universe moves in.... well, that pretty much speaks for itself.

The truth I am discovering more and more each day is that as I move out of the picture and become more fully immersed in Him, there is an unbroken channel for Him to pour out His Spirit, and give me the power I need to carry out His will.

"And you will receive POWER....!"

CHAPTER 4

Unlocking The Door

"When it was evening on that day, the first day of the week, and the doors of the house where the disciples had met were locked for fear of the Jews,...." (John 20:19 NIV)

When I was a kid, I had a brother who liked to play tricks on me. I remember clearly one particular instance that probably has had more effect on how warped I am today than any other. One of my jobs around the house was to collect the trash and take it out to the large outdoor trash cans beside the house. The collecting part was no problem. I would scurry around the house, and in five minutes have everything jammed into one or two trash cans ready to be carried outside. The problem came when I had to take the trash from the inside of the house and put it into the larger cans on the outside. The problem was not the work. The problem was that I was scared of the dark and there was no light where the outside cans were located. We had a large street light in our front yard, but its light did not reach the area where the cans were located. If anything, the eerie light from that lone street light worked its way around the corner of the house, and made the trash can area even spookier and more ominous than if there were no light.

As I look back, I do not know why it did not occur to me to take the trash out during the day. I probably would be a lot more psychologically stable if I had. Since I did not take the trash out during the day, I was faced, twice a week, with my mad, nighttime dash to the trash cans. In order to keep the "boogie man" from getting me, my biweekly ritual for seven years was always the same: I would line up on the edge of the carport light, get in my sprinter's stance, and in the blink of an eye get to the cans, empty my cargo, and zip back into the lights!

The incident with my brother took place when I was around 12 or 13 years old. It was a dark and gloomy night. There were no stars, and someone had decided to turn off the moon. My family had just finished listening to the evening news where we had heard a report about a dangerous convict who had escaped from the local prison and was at large in the city. The authorities did not want to alarm anyone, but they strongly encouraged everyone to lock their doors and windows before going to bed. Needless to say, I was not thrilled at the prospect of taking out the trash *that* night. But since the trash was going to be collected the next morning, I had no other choice. I collected my "treasure," lined up on the edge of the carport light, shot out of my sprinter's blocks, emptied my cans in record time, started my bolt back to the house.....

Oh! Did I mention that on the side of the house near the trash cans there was a large area of shrubs?!

Some of you are smiling right now! How cruel!

Yep! My loving brother decided *that* night was going to be the night he would "warp" me!

While I was collecting the trash, he made his way out the door and hid in the shrubs. As I finished emptying my cans, and was heading back to the house, he lovingly jumped out and screamed at the top of his lungs! I have heard of people having unbelievable physical strength in times of sheer terror. The only thing I wish I could keep from that night was what I did physically. I jumped 20 feet in the air and 20 feet out. I cupped my hands over my head and laid there screaming until...... I recognized the unmistakable sound of my brother laughing. There I was having a massive coronary at the age of 12, and he was having the time of his life.

What happened to my brother? After my father stopped laughing, he got a good "talking to".

How does this story relate to the opening scripture? FEAR!! Pure, unadulterated, paralyzing, lie down, and shake like a baby fear. Though I can not relate to everything the disciples were experiencing the night they had locked themselves up for "fear of the Jews", I can relate to fear and its paralyzing effect. I would like to be able to say that my debilitating fear was over something more monumental and significant than the dark. But, in a way, I can begin to appreciate the fear that was keeping the disciples locked behind closed doors.

At least the disciples had real threats to be concerned about. The religious leaders and synagogue rulers had seen the miracles, experienced the love and power, and heard Jesus teaching, but *still* did everything they could to railroad him and have him killed. They were afraid of what they did not understand and what threatened their position. If it could happen to Jesus, it could just as easily happen to his followers. The disciples knew it. I would have locked the door too. In fact, the same thing *did* ultimately happen to the disciples. The only one to escape a torturous death was John. The rest were beheaded, crucified, and martyred. Jesus even warned them that they would be hated and persecuted because of him; "If the world hates you, keep in mind that it hated me first." (John 15:18) Their fears were well-grounded.

You can almost picture the disciples behind those locked doors. In one corner was a group huddled together trying to figure out some way to sneak out of the city. Another two or three were telling about their adventures getting to the meeting. The rumors were flying concerning the extent and amount of the bounty on their heads. Every group jumped, every heart skipped at the slightest sound or disturbance in the street. Jesus had told them after his resurrection to go out and preach the news about him. The disciples were to heal the sick, cast out the demons, feed the pour, and change the world all in the name of Jesus. RIGHT! Can you hear them saying, "He's got to be kidding!" "They're out to get us. The last thing I'm going to do is show my face, much less draw attention to myself."

They were scared.

"The doors were locked for *fear* of the Jews."

The doors to that room were not the only things which were locked. The gates of the Kingdom and what *could be* in the disciples' lives were also locked up tight behind fear, apprehension, and uncertainty. Can you relate to any of their debilitating fear? When the thought crosses your mind about going out into the streets in the name of Jesus, do you feel a knot well up in your throat and a weakness in your knees? I used to, and admittedly still do at times.

A few years ago I led a Lay Speakers class in my area. After about two or three hours of instruction and discussion, I asked if anyone had any questions. One lady raised her hand and said, "Personally, I was looking forward to being a Lay Speaker....until I took this class. Now I'm not all that excited."

Let me tell you, that really boosts a teacher's ego. I asked her why she felt that way.

She said, "What you are putting before us is very threatening. You're challenging us to be like....*real* ministers for Christ. That's scary."

After a few, "That's right!" and an "Uh Huh!" or two from the rest of the group, we started talking about some of the things that kept us huddled in fear in our upper rooms.

One of the first locks mentioned was the fear of **failure**. One lady said, "What if I do it wrong? What if someone can do it better? What if I blow it and turn someone off to Jesus?"

Another person mentioned the fear of **ridicule**. He said, "I don't want anyone to think I'm a religious fanatic or a 'Jesus freak'."

Another gentleman added, "I've been going to my church for years. If I make a dramatic stand for Christ, my personal life is going to come under close scrutiny. I have too many skeletons in the closet."

Embarrassment was the third fear mentioned. The lady who mentioned this one said, "I don't know enough Bible. What if I get in a situation where I'm not able to answer the questions people ask me? And what will my friends in the Garden Society think if I'm hanging out down town with the riffraff?"

Along with all of these other "cheerful" topics (*sarcasm intended*) we talked about the prospect of **persecution** or of possibly losing a job because of a stand for Christ. We honestly discussed Christ's calling as being **inconvenient** and a call that disrupts our comfortable lives and our set schedules. For a good hour or so we shared the fears which kept our faith locked behind the closed, safe doors of "My faith is a personal thing."

Does any of this sound familiar? Do you recognize the fear? Are you standing behind the same cold, locked doors you have been standing behind for years for "fear of ......whatever?" Want to know how to unlock the doors?

Take a wild guess!

Time's up!

It's when we get out of the picture and are immersed in the Spirit of God. Only then will we ever get out of the door, down into the streets, and *live*!

The Scriptures support this fact. Jesus appeared to the disciples after his resurrection! He clearly showed them that he had conquered death. Because of Jesus' death, resurrection, and the disciples' *unquestionable knowledge* that Jesus was exactly who he said he was, they were saved. Yes, you read it right! The disciples were saved. Their acceptance of Jesus' sacrifice for their sins and his defeat of death through the resurrection had made available to them new life. BUT... But what? But where do we find them at the end of the book of John? Fishing! After their great salvation experience, because of Peter's suggestion, they decide to go back home and do some "worm casting". Read the account! It is in John 21.

Acts 2 finds the disciples still lounging around in the upper rooms. Why? First of all because Jesus told them to wait (Acts 1:4). I would guess secondly, however, because they were still scared to death to show their faces. Until.....

Until they were filled with the power and the presence of the Holy Spirit! Here is the account from the second chapter of Acts:

"When the day of Pentecost had come, they were all together in one place. And suddenly from heaven there came a sound like the rush of a violent wind, and it filled the entire house where they were sitting. Divided tongues, as of fire, appeared among them, and a tongue rested on each of them. All of them were filled with the Holy Spirit and began to speak in other languages, as the Spirit gave them ability." (Acts 2:1-4)

What happened then? According to the account, they unlocked the doors, went down into the streets, pushed their way into the midst of the very people who were looking to kill them, and boldly proclaimed the good news of Jesus to a shocked crowd.

Notice who was the main spokesman for the group; Peter, of all people! Loud-mouthed, speak-before-you-act Peter stands up and says, "May I have your attention?" You can almost see one of the disciples turn toward one of the others and say, "No! Not Peter! He's going to ruin everything."

Peter stands, no longer afraid, no longer locked behind the doors of "what will people think," or "what will they do to me." Now he is free. He has started the process of getting out of the picture, of being fully immersed into the greatest love and power he would ever know, and just the first taste gives him the courage to stand up boldly and proclaim the Good News. The scripture records, "....3000 were added to their number that day." (Acts 2:41 NIV) Why? Because the chains of fear had been broken!

For years I wallowed around behind closed doors waiting to be set free. Oh, I knew the grace of God that saved me through Christ. I had been "washed in the blood" and been made new. That "being made new" was a wonderful experience and the momentum of that experience pushed me forward for some time. It wasn't until I later began to consciously open my life to the filling of God's Spirit that I received the courage to unlock the doors which crippled my faith and began to experience all that God had in store for me.

Let me share with you a wonderful picture parallel which I experienced a few years ago. It happened during the summer of 1989 when I took my first back-packing trip. I was to be an adult assistant for a group which takes youth on week-long trips on the Appalachian Trail in southwestern Virginia. One particular night we were staying at a camp site on the summit of "Straight Mountain". The campsite was a beautiful combination of meadows and deep forest. We were having such a great time fellowshipping and worshipping God that I did not realize that it had already gotten dark. The getting dark part was not the problem. There were plenty of people around to help me feel "macho" and the noise level probably would have scared away any of the dangerous, blood-thirsty critters I knew were lurking in the shadows. The problem started around 10:30 p.m. when it suddenly dawned on me that I had not gotten ready to "hit the sack" yet.

The problem was that I have the unusual neurosis of not being able to climb into a sleeping bag with a day's worth of grime and trail sweat on my body. Somewhere, somehow, I was going to have to get cleaned up.

I knew I did not have enough water in my canteens to clean up and still have some to drink the next day. I remembered the spring we had used earlier that day to pump water. I knew that I could get a good sponge bath, fill my canteen again, and have plenty of water for the next day to boot. I picked up my flashlight and my little trail rag, -some people call it a towel- and set off down the path to the spring.

An important part of this story is that one of the principles of back-packing is, "Pack it in. Pack it out." If you go back-packing, you are carrying everything on your back for five or six days. So, a smart back-packer shoots for *no weight*! That goes for flashlights as well! Since you only stay up one or two hours after dark, there is really no need to bring a *large* flashlight. Since there is no need for a flashlight, a "smart packer" brings the *lightest* light he or she can find. I had a *small* light! I think lightening bugs put out more light than my little pen light! But, despite the oppressive odds, grime was winning out over fear. I decided to take my chances. I knew the path to the spring was celar and well marked. The spring was only a half mile from the campsite and, I thought to myself, "For goodness sake you wimp. You're supposed to be a man." So, off I went.

At first, everything was fine. I soon noticed, though, that there was just enough moon to make the shadows a little more "lively" than usual and because of that, I have to admit, I was a little jumpy. I was making my way down the trail without any mishaps until.... you guessed it, until my flashlight went out about a quarter of the way from the spring. There I stood, in the middle of the dark woods, almost a good half mile from camp, by myself, with the "pen light from Satan." What to do? I could not yell for help. I did have *some* dignity to preserve. Since I was so close to the spring, I did not want to go back without washing up. So, summoning all of my manliness, and knowing that I was near my destination, I started walking toward the spring until I heard the "splash, splash, splashing" of my feet in the creek.

It goes without saying, that night I took the fastest sponge bath in history. Once I finished, then came the truly exciting part, the walk back.

The good news was, that by the time I had finished sponging, my eyes had adjusted to the darkness. There was just enough moon for me to see the trail head and begin my trek back. Everything was going just "hunky dory" until I ran into a bush. I thought to myself, "This bush wasn't here earlier. I don't remember there being a bush in the middle of the path this afternoon when we came for water. I know no one planted it just recently. OOPS. I believe I am off the path."

Actually, that is probably not a direct quote. To be quite honest, I was about to lose my cookies. I was lost!!! My worst nightmare had come true. Even if I could have put aside my pride and yelled, I was too far away from the camp for anyone to have heard me. Only for a minute did I think about going on and trying to find my way out, but I decided that would not be a good idea. It was not that I was such an experienced back-packer and that I knew better than to try and find my way out in the dark. I just did not *want* to! I could have laid down where I was and let them find my dried up corpse the next day!

Hey! I was getting hysterical!

Then suddenly this thought blasted through all of the internal screams and "what ifs". "Pray!"

Pray! Now there's an option I had not thought of up to that point! So, what did I do? I prayed! Boy howdy, did I pray! And almost as fast as the panic had set in, a calm rushed over my soul and soothed my spirit. I even closed my eyes in order to drink in the wonderful presence I was experiencing. I really do not know how long I stood there and prayed. All I know is when I opened my eyes, I was at peace and I knew I was not alone.

What now?

Try and keep all of the details straight: I had not been teleported to the campsite, and it was still dark. In other words, the situation had not really changed at all. I was still off the trail, my light was still out, and the sun had not miraculously appeared. It just so happened that my head was turned in just the right direction to see a break in the bushes, THE PATH! I bounded through the weeds and bushes until I found myself standing on the straight and narrow once again. I shouted a quick "Amen" and headed back to camp.

The crazy thing is, that as I was making my way back, I noticed a large spider web over to the left which had been covered with the evening dew. With the moonlight hitting it just right, it was a beautiful sight. I stopped for a second to admire the intricacy of the spider's work and marvel at God's creation. Then it hit me: "What in the world am I doing?!" I thought to myself.

"It's still dark! I still don't have a working flashlight. I still have a good hike ahead of me. Am I nuts?"

"Nope!" came the answer. "You are Mine."

There I stood, immersed in The Presence which not only took me beyond the *fears* of the moment, but in the midst of a fearful situation, allowed me to see the beauty I would have otherwise missed.

The happy ending of the story is this: I have not been back behind those locked doors of the fear of the dark since that time. In fact, the last time I looked, I think those particular doors were literally blown off their hinges.

Why does God want to fill us with His Spirit and presence? It is the only way we will ever get out of our locked doors, get beyond the dark forests, and out into the streets for Him!

Fear in Christian Living

My story of the woods is true, dramatic, and paints a picture of how literally being immersed in the presence of God can take us beyond our fears and into the light.

But what about fears like the disciples faced? What about the fear so many experience when they are faced with a situation which calls them to share their faith? What about public prayer? What about standing up for what you think is right, despite opposing odds? Does getting out of the picture take us beyond these fears? My answer is a resounding, "YES!"

I have never had a problem sharing my faith or proclaiming the Gospel of Jesus to a crowd, leading study groups, or teaching Sunday School. In fact, I feel somewhat comfortable in front of a crowd. However, when I first started the process of becoming a minister, I discovered that I had a *real* problem when I went before a group of my peers. The first glimpse of this problem came when I experienced what my seminary called a "professional assessment." In short, this is when a ministerial candidate meets with about five other ministers and is asked to articulate his/her faith. Without *any* exaggeration at all, when I went before this group of peers, my mind would turn to mush, I would lose 15 pounds in sweat, and most of the synapses between my mouth and my cerebral cortex would break.

I will probably always remember my Professional Assessment experience. After my impressive "performance", I was not surprised that the overall recommendation from the committee was that I get some counseling as well as take a few classes based on the teachings of a few recommended theologians. "It appears", they said as one voice, "that you have a problem articulating your faith. We think you need to do some more study."

Well, of course I had trouble "articulating my faith." My mouth was in the room and my brain had taken an emergency flight to the Bahamas.

My next encounter with my brain going on vacation was when I went for my Deacon's orders. "Going for one's Deacon's orders" consists of writing a few papers on prescribed subjects and then discussing them with a number of "interviewing committees". Of course these committees were also made up of a group of my peers.

My first committee dealt with my "calling" into the ministry. Their job was to see how well I could articulate my faith and calling from God. I was sitting on the edge of the circle when one wonderfully loving, older pastor turned to me with a very genuine smile on his face and said, "Tell us about grace."

"Grace! What's grace!" my mind screamed! I sat there frantically trying to pull up the files on grace from my brain. It seemed my brain had burned those files just before it went this time to Acapulco. All I could think of was the title of a

Christian book I had read years before, <u>Grace is not a blue eyed blond</u>.

The gentleman who had asked me the question noticed I was turning a very decorative shade of green. He put his hand lightly on my shoulder and said, "Calm down. We're here *for* you. Not against you. Take a deep breath and think." Somehow, by the grace of God, I made it through those committees. As far as I can remember, I don't believe they recommended counseling this time. That was a relief.

It was the same in every similar situation. My body would go before one of those review committees and my mind would go to Disney World. After every experience like that, I would ask my wife the same question: "What in the world is going on?! Why do I have such a difficult time in these interviews?" The answer was simple. I was *afraid*! I was afraid of what they might think. I was afraid of failure. I was afraid I would embarrass myself. I was afraid that I would not appear as smart and as intelligent as the others on the committee or the candidates who had come before me. I was afraid I wouldn't be considered a success by simply breezing through all of the requirements. I was afraid. And, that fear kept what God had been sharing with me and showing me over the years locked up behind closed doors . I knew what I believed. Sure, there were -and still are- unanswered questions and doubts in my mind. But I knew in *Whom* I believed. Yet fear of a particular group was keeping my testimony from ever being expressed.

Then one day, years later, the concept of being immersed in the Spirit of God finally began to sink in and start to become a reality in my life. Now I can boldly testify, "The fear is gone!" Why the difference? It's simple: if I am out of the picture and if God is the focus, then who cares what they think about me.... and God can take care of Himself. Oh, I still get a little nervous every now and then, but I no longer have a debilitating fear when faced with a group of my peers. In fact, when given the opportunity to address my peers, like the spider web on the trail, I almost relish the moment and enjoy the experience.

The reality taking place in my life and in my soul is best expressed by the apostle Paul, "It is no longer I who live, but Christ lives in me." (Galatians 2:20)

Why has God designed it so that we are immersed in His Spirit? Because the foundation of fear is the possibility of *self* being injured or harmed. If, like Paul, I can say, "To live is Christ, to die is gain." (Phillipians 1:21), and like Jesus say, "Thy will be done." (Matthew 26:42), *self* is no longer *the* focus, God is. If that is true in your life, then consequently fear is defeated.

CHAPTER 5
Finding Value

"here is no remembrance of men of old, and even those who are yet to come will not be remembered by those who follow. I have seen all the things that are done under the sun; all of them are meaningless, a chasing after the wind." *(Ecclesiastes 1:11,14 NIV)*

How do you feel about yourself right now? Good? Bad? Indifferent?

This morning, when you were getting ready for the day, did you pause in front of the mirror to admire the view and think, "Wow! You're a good lookin' critter!?" While you stole a quick look at your reflection did you wonder why mothers all over the world don't hide their children's eyes when they see you coming? Have you reflected on your life recently? How do the results of that reflection make you feel about yourself? Any great accomplishments? Do you have anything worthy of writing "Ripley's Believe It or Not"? Have you made an earth shattering difference in this world and now are concerned about who is going to take up the slack when you are gone? Feel good, OR, do you wonder why God wasted skin on you. Do you often parallel yourself in cosmic importance with things like naval fuzz and head lice?

How do you feel about yourself today?

I'm asking, "How do you feel about yourself," not just to have you do a little thinking about the answer. It *does* behoove us every once in awhile to ask it. *The* reason I'm asking "How do you feel about yourself" is to get you thinking about *how you decide* the answer. In other words, what criteria do you use, by what gauge do you measure yourself in order to decide how you feel about yourself, how you're doing, or if you are of any value at all?

39

Let me offer a few criteria I have used and have seen used by others over the years to decide the question of worth and value.

OTHERS

I guess the most influential criteria we use to measure our value or worth is *what people say about us* -both verbally and non-verbally. If this is your number one, I can almost guarantee that how you feel about yourself is one big roller coaster ride which has many more valleys than it does highs. But join the club. For whatever reason, most people look to others to help establish their sense of values. Why this is the case, I have no idea.

Think how ridiculous it is to say that how you feel about yourself depends on whether Janie Lou Armblop smiles at you from across the room or your co-workers give you pats on the back. Would you want someone to base their self worth on what *you* say about them? I wouldn't! I wouldn't because I am not qualified to make those judgments. If we are not qualified to judge others, then why do we rely so heavily on other's judgment of us?!

Go figure!

FAMILY

We may feel good or bad about ourselves depending on what our *family* says about us.

Many of us look to our families because we believe that the persons who are related to us are wonderful and all-knowing. They're related to us aren't they? Since these persons are so perfect, their opinion should matter more than just the average Joe off the street or even Janie Lou Armblop. I hate to throw this bug in your soup, but those persons whom we call, "Mom," "Dad," "Grandma," "Sis," "Unk", are someone else's Janie Lou Armblop, co-worker, or average Joe off the street. They are just as confused as the rest of the human race.

Though our family's opinion is important, finding our value in their opinion of us is just as dangerous as finding it in any other member of the human race. Hey! Let's face it, people's opinion can change. They change depending on the weather, health factors, and that person's own feelings about himself. Let's take a bold step and throw out OTHERS as an option for finding our self worth.

STYLE

We could measure our sense of worth by whether we are in *style* or not.

Pardon me while I roll on the floor in uncontrollable laughter! Rely on *style* for my sense of worth?! Good luck! We could go to any stylish store today and buy what the popular magazines and popular people of our society say is "in style" and I can guarantee those very same clothes will be "geeky" this time next year. If not next week! Of course, if you waited 20 years, those same clothes would be back in style again. That is beside the point, though. The point is, there is no style. Or at least there is no style that *lasts*!

The strange thing is that even though we know the truth about styles, we still rush out to buy the latest fad in a vain attempt to look like all the other malnourished models gracing the front of glamour magazines. It's ridiculous! If styles constantly change, I vote we throw "being in style" out as a criteria for judging our value.

LOOKS

What about *looks*? A gauge for our worth second only to others is the criteria of how we look. We would like to think that this shallow method of judging one's worth is only relevant to teenagers and younger adults, but a quick glance at our society show that's not the case. Though there probably are more people who use looks as a criteria in the younger age group, they hardly monopolize it. If the teen group did monopolize that criteria, cosmetics, hair coloring, hair replacement plans, wrinkle removers, and so on, would not be among *the* biggest industries in the country.

We need to admit that all too many of us use looks as a gauge to decide whether we are of value or not. It's sad.

If you are one of the millions who have jumped on the "how do I look?" band wagon, let me put your mind at ease. If you are good looking now, enjoy it. According to what the "world" (and especially America) says, you won't be good looking for long. Your good looks will fade over the years. Though I personally would debate the belief that "younger is prettier," it is the prevailing opinion our society has adopted as the truth. If, on the other hand, you are not very good looking, HEY! hang in there. According to interviews with the same people who wear their pants down to their knees, still live at home, and don't know which way a baseball cap is supposed to face, all persons over the age of 50 look alike anyway.

Since there is no consistent opinion about what looks good and *when* it looks good, looks would also not be a very reliable gauge of worth.

THE CHURCH

How about the *church*? Is the church the place to find my sense of value and worth? Though I am a minister, I would emphatically say, "NOPE!" Churches are just as wishy-washy and confused as everyone else about a person's worth.

Take the movement of "I'm OK. You're OK" which caught on like wild fire in the 70's. That movement within and outside of the church was saying to us, "Perk up! You're all right! No one is flawed. No one really has problems if we just stick together." The movement focused on people feeling good about themselves, but did little to bring about a person having a lasting sense of value.

There are, of course, groups within the church whose focus is the other extreme espoused by all "real, true Christians." The flip side of the "I'm OK" movement is the teaching that says, "You should feel bad about yourself. God designed it that way. All of us are scum and sinners, destined to damnation if not for the grace of God. If you feel good about yourself. Stop it! That's not the Christian way!"

If we can't even decide in the church what the gauge is for a person's value, I say we throw out the mixed messages of the church as the *ultimate* criteria.

POSSESSIONS

There are those of course who will support the "American way" and suggest we find our true value in what we own.... *our possessions.*

Finding our value through our possessions is so shallow and short-sighted it's really not worth spending a great deal of time on.

One of *the* reasons I would not recommend basing your value on what you possess is that you may not always possess these things. Jesus said it best, "Do not store up for yourselves treasures on earth, where moth and rust destroy, and where thieves break in and steal." (Matthew 6:19) What we possess today, we may not possess tomorrow.

ACCOMPLISHMENTS

Lastly, many of us base our sense of value and worth on what we have *accomplished* in our lives. Simply put, if we have done something noteworthy in our lives, then we feel good about ourselves. If, according to some vague criteria, we haven't accomplished anything of any significance, then we head off like a middle-aged man in a mid-life crisis looking for excitement and change in an attempt to dull our sense of value*less*ness.

The ridiculous thing is that even if we *do* accomplish something of any significance in our lives, it really does not seem to make us feel very valuable and worthy. Why? Simple: When you talk with someone who has accomplished some significant things in their lives, what most often do they talk about? They talk about *themselves* or their great accomplishment. Why? Why brag? If they have done great things and feel good about themselves, why push it on others? Because these persons who have done "great things" are the only ones who remember their "significant accomplishment" and want to make sure that others -who really don't care- are constantly reminded.

It seems that the writer of Ecclesiastes was right concerning the criteria we tend to use in finding value in ourselves, "All is meaningless, a chasing after the wind." (Ecclesiastes 1:14b)

Can you relate to any of these struggles? Have you tried to find your self-value by standing on any of these shifting sands? I have.

I am thrilled to let you know that my "worthless zone" days are no more. I have begun to discover a sense of worth and value that will forever be unshakable. If you ask me today how I feel about myself, I can say, "Valuable!"

What made the difference?

If you were sitting next to me right now, and knew about my ministerial situation, you might think it is because the ministries that I am involved with today are going pretty well. I would have to admit that I am finally beginning to understand what my father meant when he talked about ministry being fun. God *is* using my life in some significant ways to bring about some obvious results. It does feel good. But..... Make sure you are paying attention. I want you to get the next line. What is happening to me now has little, if anything, to do with my sense of value and worth!

What had made the difference?

God finally got through. I have begun to understand and experience what Paul meant when he said to the men of Athens, "For in him (*Christ*) we live and move and have our being." (Acts 17:28) Simply put, I find my value in being God's..... **period**! Why did God design it so that we should be out of the picture? Because it is only *then* that we find true value and worth; when we find it in God *alone*!

Take a look at what Paul is saying in Acts 17:28a. First of all he is saying that in God, and because of God, Paul lives and breathes. All that he is, literally the breath he takes, he takes because of God. "I live." Paul says.

".....And move," Paul continues. Literally he is saying, "I am moved." In other words, for Paul, God is the wind beneath his wings. God is the current which steers the boat. There are no other influences for Paul but God. He is saying, "If I move, it is because God moved me."

"I live and am moved and have my being." The "have my being" part is a nice scholarly way of translating what Paul was saying. If you took what Paul said and translated it literally, it would read, "In him I live, am moved, and **IS**!" Paul is saying that because God is, Paul is. You can't get any more basic than that. We find lasting and real value for who we are only when we find it in God! Trying to find self-value in anything else is like scooping up a handful of water from a creek and trying to run inside to show it to your family. The scooping part is great. At least ten to twenty feet away from the creek, you are still excited. But by the time you hit the front door of your house, all you have to show for all your troubles are damp hands and air. Only in God will we find self-worth which lasts.

Awareness of Reality

I have also discovered that the closer I move to being immersed in God and finding my value in Him alone, the more I am acquiring a keen awareness of reality.

Let me illustrate what I mean by "an awareness of *reality*."

Imagine Preacher Windowpain whose self-worth is based on the gauge of *accomplishments*. The problem is Preacher Windowpain has not yet, by human standards, accomplished "great things" in his ministry. Because of his lack of accomplishments, he feels a little inadequate.

Located on the other side of the valley, is another preacher whose church is growing like gangbusters. Everybody in the area is talking about what is going on at Little Twig Church of the Road Kill. The preacher there, Preacher Joe Snively, has a reputation of being a great speaker and administrator. With these two churches in such close proximity, what do you think is running through the mind of Preacher Windowpain about Preacher Snively and the happenings at Little Twig? Speaking from vast experience as an insecure minister, I can safely say, "Probably not good stuff."

In order to justify the lack of growth in his own church, Preacher Windowpain might play with thoughts like: "Little Twig is in a growing area. I'm serving a church in a mill town. What can I expect? Preacher Snively might be selling out the Gospel in order to get new members. I could fill a church, too, if I was willing to turn it into a social club! I'm going to stay true to the Gospel no matter what!"

You get the point. Preacher Windowpain is not really concerned with reality and how things *are*. He is more concerned with how he wished things were in order to raise his "accomplishments gauge" a notch or two.

An awareness of reality for Preacher Windowpain would mean two things: 1) He would be willing to admit that he is not God's sole answer to the ministry and that there are, and will continue to be, other ministers who are much more gifted than he. Most importantly, 2) He *has been* used by God if only he would get out of his self-pitying pool of drivel and look. If it were not for preacher Windowpain's sensitivity, little Jim Johnson never would have given his life to Jesus last year. If it were not for Preacher Windowpain, Widow Andrews would have never been visited all winter long, nor would she have had a special surprise from the "Seekers" Sunday school class who helped winterize the little shack she calls a house.

Though Preacher Windowpain has not been used to move mountains, there has been a hill or two which God moved because of his availability. A keen awareness of reality is being willing to admit, "I *do* have some gifts and graces. I *do* have some strengths and abilities. And, I also have some problems and weaknesses as well." Those in the know call that *humility*. Humility.... possibly another word for God inspired reality.

Appreciation For Others

If Preacher Windowpain could find his value in God alone, and *if* he was consequently enabled to see reality a little more clearly, Preacher Windowpain would also be given the wonderful gift of being able to look across the valley to Little Twig church of the Road Kill and *celebrate* with Preacher Spivey the movement of God in the midst of that church. Speaking from personal experience, that has been one of the most freeing and refreshing aspects of finding my value in God; i.e. My growing ability to *truly* celebrate with a brother or sister minister and appreciate the value of their ministry.

Less Stress

Another benefit of finding my value in God is that I discovered the stress level in my life fell off dramatically.

You might be wondering what does finding one's value in God have to do with one's stress level. Good question. The picture which has stayed in my mind is of a doll that was popular back in the mid 80's. The selling point of this doll was that it was made of a rubber which could be pulled, and pulled. The commercial always showed about four people stretching this doll in four different directions until it looked like it was about to snap into a thousand pieces. Doesn't that sound like our life styles today?

How many of you this past week have complained to someone about the enormous demands on your time and attention? There is work, family, social issues, and the church

clamoring for your time. Each one of them is saying, "Here!
This is what is really important!"

"If you were a good employee, *this* would be the
number one priority for you!"

"If you were a good parent/spouse, *this* would be the
number one priority for you!"

"If you were a good American, *this* would be the
number one priority for you!"

"If you were a good Christian, *this* would be the
number one priority for you!"

Can you hear the voices? With a slight change of a
familiar ad used by McDonalds, "Have you had your guilt
today?" It is the voices which cause the stress. Which one do
we listen to? Which one is the priority? How do we limit the
stress? The answer is: Put a priority on *one* voice.... The
Voice. If I find my value in God, and if I can hear what
direction God thinks is the priority at that time, then the choice
is only, "Do I follow or not?" Every other question is
irrelevant.

Perseverance

Once we begin to find our self-worth in God alone, we
can experience an ever increasing *inner fortitude*. In other
words, we begin to have a greater capacity to stand for what is
inspired by God and to *persevere* in our stand.

Ask yourself this question: "Why do we quit?" "Why
do we quit anything?"

Sometimes we quit simply because things are getting
too difficult. If we are trying to dig a five foot hole in solid
rock on a 95 degree day and there is no shade in sight, we may
"hang it up" because it's not worth the trouble.

Sometimes we quit because we are quitters. There are
those who never finish anything because the following
philosophy of life was ingrained into them at some point by
some other shallow person: "When the going gets tough,....

quit!" If that is our credo for life, we will rarely keep working until the hard-to-accomplish things are done.

Most of the time we tend to quit because it looks like failure is inevitable. To a degree, quitting *then* does make some sense. If there is no way we are going to succeed at some project, no matter how hard or how long we work, then what is the use of continuing? Exercise is a good example. If we have worked for years to lose those pounds and get into shape, with little if any results, why not quit? If a job looks and possibly *is* impossible, why not quit? If we don't quit, we would be wasting our time while we *could be* doing something more productive.

If you don't agree that people tend to quit when failure looks inevitable, think about the other side of the spectrum. Have you ever seen anyone quit when the finish line was in view? When an able-bodied runner sees the finish line, the desire to complete the race is increased. The adrenaline pumps! She can hear her heart beating in her ears, and she pushes forward with renewed enthusiasm, ready to complete the task at hand. Rarely does anyone quit when success is guaranteed. We quit because the job is impossible, the finish line is nowhere to be seen, and there is no use in going on..... At least I used to think that was the case. When we find our value in God, we also acquire the ability to keep going on, even in the face of inevitable failure.

Why? Does it have something to do with the fact that God gives us strength to press on and if we are faithful, we *will* ultimately be successful. I think that is the case at times. But that has more to do with the chapter on "Power" than it does in finding one's value in God.

The truth that I have begun to discover, the perseverance I have begun to experience, comes from the fact that if I find my value in God, regardless of the situation or struggle I face, I am in a win-win situation. To put it quite pointedly, *I can't lose*!

Think about these facts: 1) If I hear only God's voice and follow His leading, God is faithful to use me. 2) If I am getting out of the picture, experiencing God's presence and power, then what was at one time seemingly impossible, will become possible. BUT, 3) Even if by the world's standards we apparently fail, the ultimate (eternal) gauge for my actions is: "Did I remain faithful and connected to God?" There is nothing, especially on the eternal scale of things, which is more important. So, if through my apparent failure I become even more surrendered to God and even less in the picture,.... **I WIN!!**

When we are getting out of the picture, we begin to find our value in God alone. Oh, what wonders are in store for us then!

CHAPTER 6

The music is never heard unless the Maestro plays the strings

"Andrew, Simon Peter's brother, spoke up, 'Here is a boy with five small barley loaves and two small fish, but how far will they go among so many?.... Jesus then took the loaves, gave thanks, and distributed to those who were seated as much as they wanted. He did the same with the fish.

When they had all had enough to eat, he said to his disciples, 'Gather the pieces that are left over. Let nothing be wasted.' So they gathered them and filled twelve baskets with the pieces of the five barley loaves left over by those who had eaten." (John 6:8-13 NIV)

When I was in seminary, I was having some real problems with some of the things which *were* -and especially were *not*- being taught. I remember daily seeking to hear the words that would keep me focused on what I was there to be trained to do, instead of listening to group after group of seminarians waste more and more time debating totally inconsequential topics. I wanted to be able to stand up and say, "You people are off the mark. Who cares how many angels can dance on the point of a pen! *This* is what the message of Christ's Good News is!"

That is what I wanted to say, but it was the *"this"* portion that I was having trouble finding words to express.

Then one evening I was sitting in my study at home trying to get through another boring text book on hypothetical theology, when -wonders of wonders- my mind began to wander. In an attempt to get refocused, I looked up from my book, set my glasses over to the side, and stared blankly across the room. While I was staring, I noticed an old rocking chair sitting in the corner with my guitar propped against it. It had been at least a year since I had drawn anything, so I decided to kill some time by trying my hand at sketching the rocking chair and guitar. With pencil and paper in hand, I produced a pretty good drawing in about 30 minutes. I held it out at arm's length to admire my wonderful talents, and complimented myself on still "having it." When I laid the picture down, these words came to mind, "The music is never heard, unless the Maestro plays the strings."

I said, "What?! Where in the world did that come from?"

The words came back again. No question about it, I was almost hearing an audible voice in my head. The voice said again, "The music is never heard unless the Maestro plays the strings."

I quickly turned the picture over and jotted the words down. I set my pencil over to the side and continued to stare at the phrase, "The music is never heard unless the Maestro plays the strings." Then it hit me!! I had spent a lot of time looking for some deep intellectual explanation of Christ's Good News to share with my peers in Seminary. I wanted to make "it" intellectually stimulating.... not to mention impressive. But here it was in those simple words. In the midst of all the debate and discussion about what makes a successful minister, what promotes church growth, what constitutes a dynamic sermon, and the all important: How in the world do you fill out a year end report for the conference? The message of Jesus was: "The music is never heard unless the Maestro plays the strings."

The point is this: *WE* can pick up the guitar -our lives, our churches, our missions- and pluck the strings until our fingers bleed. *We* can play with sincere commitment and unlimited talent until our hands are numb. *We* can take all the training and absorb all the instruction the "experts" have to share with us. *We* can analyze and take a course on music appreciation. *We* can have all the instruments at our disposal spit-polished and in mint condition. There will be no music, however, if *we* are the ones doing the playing. The only way there will ever be music which soothes the soul, changes the world, and gives testimony to The Light will be when the instrument is surrendered to The Maestro, The Spirit of God, and *He* strums the strings.

Another result of being immersed in the Spirit of God and "getting out of the picture" is that our lives begin to **SING**!!

Honestly speaking, there was a time in my life when Jim wanted to be in charge. I wanted to call the shots and I was going to do whatever was necessary to be successful. I knew God was the answer to life, and that He was able to work through my bumbling and stumbling efforts despite me. But, sadly, because **I** was playing the strings, often there was just an irritating noise being produced from my life *and* my ministry instead of beautiful Gospel music.

As far as churches being the strings to play, I have had some pretty good strings. The churches that I have served have all had great people, and the areas had at least *some* potential. The problem was that if **I** wasn't the one playing the strings, then *the people* were. Granted, every once in awhile some decent sounds were made. There were enough sounds made that some of the people in the area stopped to see what was going on. And again, God, by his wondrous grace, worked through us, despite us. But, for every few minutes of music *we* made, there were hours of.... irritating noise!

If you are getting tired of my church illustrations, I'll use marriage as an example.

There was a gentleman I met a few years ago who shared with me that when he first married, he had read all the books one is supposed to read before one gets married. Because of all the reading, he had a very analytical concept of what needed to be done in order to have a successful marriage. I guess you could say he went into marriage like baking a cake. If he put in the right ingredients and followed the directions, a perfect marriage cake would appear. By his own admission, *he* was going to be playing the strings.

His wife will be the first one to attest that their first year was not the greatest. He was completely befuddled -new word- because he was doing all the things he thought he was supposed to do, but few things were working out like he had planned. Though there were fleeting moments of music, much of what they heard was noise. Both of them were able to say on their second anniversary that they had experienced *four* really good months of marriage. There was a day there, and a week here where music was heard. But, primarily because *they* were playing the strings, most of what was heard was noise.

Finally, they immersed their relationship in God. They handed the stressed and stretched strings over to Him and allowed Him to play. The result? MUSIC!

The best example of the music made when the strings are played by The Maestro is two persons I knew during my years of higher education. When I was in seminary, there was a gentleman who had everything going for him. He was handsome. He made straight A's every semester. He was gifted in music and played the piano beautifully. He could sing like an angel, and to top it all off, he was a wonderful speaker. He could get a group's attention in seconds. It was really sickening! He was the type of guy all of us normal people wanted to take out behind the barn and pour ants down his pants.

We all assumed, if the system in our denomination remained the same, he would one day become a bishop. If not Bishop, "Ben" would probably wind up in some prestigious position somewhere. And he would wind up there because *that* is the song he played. Ben played songs about Ben. That is all you ever heard. With those beautiful strings at his disposal, he strummed them perfectly playing "Ode to Ben". The problem with his music was that after a few bars it was nothing but irritating noise. The strings were gifted and beautiful. But there was no music. There was nothing of any real substance. At least there wasn't when I knew him in seminary. Prayerfully he has changed.

There was another guy I knew during my college years. By worldly standards he had average strings. He had average looks (which were at least better than *my* average) and average athletic abilities. There were a number of times I had to tutor him in some subjects, and even gave him advice on how to ask out girls. (You will have to take my word for it when I say that anyone getting advice from me about girls is REALLY desperate!) "Ed" was quiet and average. He couldn't play an instrument and everyone prayed he would never sing. Ordinary strings. Not much to look at, and certainly no one from whom you would expect great things! But, *he* is not the one playing his strings. He realized years ago that if he played the strings, all anyone would hear would be noise. So, he handed all of his mediocre strings over to the Maestro. Oh, the beautiful music his life is making today. As I write, he is a missionary in China....sharing the music.

"The music is never heard unless the Maestro plays the strings."

The following poem says it best. Perhaps it will speak to you as well.

'Twas battered and scarred, and the auctioneer
Thought it scarcely worth his while
To waste much time on the old violin,
But he held it up with a smile.
"What am I biddin', good folks?" he cried.
"Who'll start the biddin' for me?
A dollar? A dollar? Then two? Only Two?
Two dollars and who'll make it three?"
Three dollars once. Three dollars twice!
Going for three..., But no.
From the room far back, a gray haired man
Came forward and picked up the bow.
Then wiping the dust from the old violin,
And tightening the loosened strings,

He played a melody, pure and sweet,
As the caroling angels sing.

The music ceased, and the auctioneer,
In a voice that was quiet and low,
Said, "What am I bid for the old violin?"
And he held it up with the bow.
"A thousand dollars! And who'll make it two?
Two thousand! And who'll make it three?
Three thousand once, three thousand twice,
And going and gone!" said he.
The people cheered, but some of the cried,
"We don't quite understand.
What changed it's worth?" Swift came the reply,
"The touch of the master's hand."

And many a man with life out of tune, and battered and scarred
with sin,
Is auctioned cheap to the thoughtless crowd
Much like the old violin.
A "mess of pottage," a glass of wine;
A game -- and he travels on.
He is "going" once, and "going" twice,
He's "going" and almost "gone."
But the Master comes, and the foolish crowd
Never quite understands,
The worth of a soul and the change that is wrought
By the touch of the Master's hand.
(Author Unknown)

Are you tired of the noise? Are you ready to have some music played from your life? Keep in mind, the music played could be anything from "Mary Had A Little Lamb" to "Beethoven's Fifth Symphony". It could be anything from a gentle soothing melody which touches only a few, to a dynamic orchestral movement that rocks a continent. The point is, The Maestro is playing what *He* wants to play and what is valuable

to Him at that time.... and *that* is music, no matter how you cut
it!

Are you ready for some music?
Be immersed. Get out of the picture!

CHAPTER 7

Breaking the Elevator Syndrome

"After Jesus said this, he looked toward heaven and prayed:...... 'My prayer is not for them alone. I pray also for those who will believe in me through their message, that all of them may be one, Father, just as you are in me and I am in you. May they also be in us so that the world may believe that you have sent me.'" (John 17:1,20,21 NIV)

Elevators!   Adults hate them.   Kids love them. Whatever your personal feelings are about elevators, with the increase of high rise buildings, they have become a necessity. My most extensive exposure to elevators has been my frequent visits to see church members in the hospital.

These happy hospital elevators are consistently filled with happy hospital patrons, who seem to find unparalleled joy in stopping at every floor going up or down. I am not sure whether this compulsion to stop at every floor has to do with a malfunction in the elevator itself or if the happy hospital patrons simply want to assure themselves that each floor is still around. Either way, the elevators are packed and I regularly have ample opportunity to experience their "packedness". Of course, the highlight of my elevator experience is climbing into one of these crowded boxes and realizing that there is hardly enough room to turn around and face the door. It is then that I begin scanning the walls for the weight limit recommendations and estimating the total gross weight of my fellows passengers.

The reason I mention elevators is to point out one observation I have made over my long extended years of elevator travel: **People do not talk**. There are exceptions to every rule, but for the most part, people on elevators do not talk. They don't look down either. If I were riding in a contraption suspended by a one inch cable which could break at any time, plummeting me to certain death, I would want to know where the floor is. And I do! Every time I get into an elevator, I make sure I know where the floor is. Most people do not look at the floor though. Where do they look? The numbers! Everyone knows that the third floor is going to follow the fourth, but they keep their eyes on those numbers nonetheless. And it is always dead quiet. No one talks. No one touches. Heaven forbid someone should laugh! Everyone stays in their place and waits for their time to unload. I call this pleasant exchange among my fellow happy hospital patrons the "Elevator syndrome".

A few years ago, I read an article by a Christian writer who said that elevators are a microcosm of the world. He was right. People do not communicate anymore. Everywhere you look there is isolation, separation, one brother ignoring another brother, and it is a condensed version of what takes place all over this planet. Take a field trip this afternoon and drop by a doctor's waiting room. Stand in line at a bank for a few hours. Simply walk the streets of any city, and you will see that people do not talk, communicate, and certainly do not touch unless they have to.

I remember as a child looking forward to leaving the cities of Florida on our vacations and getting into the rural areas of Tennessee. I looked forward to traveling the country roads for the simple fact that everyone waved at us as they drove past. The first time this happened, my family thought there was something wrong with the car. Everyone kept lifting their hand off the steering wheel as they went by. We thought they might have been saying, "You have fire coming out of your car, but forget about me stopping." They were actually saying, "Howdy stranger. Glad to have you in our parts."

I have noticed, however, that in most rural areas, the tendency to wave at strangers has all but vanished. We all have fallen prey to the "Elevator Syndrome!" Most of us are wrapped up in the cocoons we have constructed in order to protect us, but which ultimately separate us from others around us.

One of the best "take a look at your own home" examples of how we intentionally isolate ourselves from one another is the presence of a television in *every* bedroom. Heaven forbid we might all want to not talk *together* while watching a mind numbing program. We want to not talk, in separate rooms, watching our *own* mind numbing programs.

You will find the Elevator Syndrome in elevators, waiting rooms, offices buildings, homes.... and I am sad to say, churches. You can see this syndrome rear its ugly head in the people who come late, slip in the back, and then slip out again during the closing hymn in order to avoid having to talk with anyone. We have our safe, non-threatening worship where no one gets carried away. We hope the minister does not say anything which will embarrass us while we keep our eyes on the bulletin, following the numbers, as the service slowly makes its way to the end and we can get out!

Not only does the *worship* in our churches encourage the Elevator Syndrome, but so do many of our "look how faithful I am" religious clichés we like to use. The one cliché in particular that I am thinking of is, "It's me and Jesus against the world." Those who use this cliché are basically saying, "I don't need you. Just give me Jesus, my Bible, a mountain to climb, and all will be right with the world."

Every time I hear "It's me and Jesus against the world" and other clichés along those lines, I think of an older gentleman in one of my previous churches. To everyone around, he was a saint. He was kind, considerate, and knew his Bible fairly well. His big declaration of faith was, "Whenever anything stands against me, it's just me and Jesus against it. Together we can overcome." Almost every time he would say that, he would puff out his chest in proud defiance of the rest of us who were so lowly in faith. Though everyone admired his apparent faith and wonderful "I can make it with Jesus" words, there was something about him that constantly raised red flags in my mind and soul. Though I knew he had a relationship with Jesus, I was not sure he knew what that relationship was all about. A few years later, I found out that my "red flags" had been justified.

The situation was this: He lost his wife of 30 years and consequently slipped into a deep depression. That's not to say that anyone who suffers a great loss and slips into depression is not strong in their faith. There was one definite, discernible cause for "Allen's" depression. His "Me and Jesus" mind-set had separated him from the rest of the body of Christ who could have been there to help him through times of struggles and trials.

You may relate to "Allen", and I can almost guarantee you know someone like him. The self-righteous "me and Jesus against the world" misunderstanding of Christianity is everywhere. The sad truth is that though Christians should be setting the standards for unity and cooperation in this world, because of people just like "Allen", we wind up perpetuating the Elevator Syndrome instead of alleviating it. The simple fact is that a part of being immersed and connected to God is being connected to everyone else who is connected to God.

Jesus prayed, "Father, make them **ONE!**" (John 17:21)

If that does not "float your boat", take a gander at what Paul has to say about the issue:

> "The body is a unit, though it is made up of many parts; and though all its parts are many, they form one body. So it is with Christ. For we were all baptized by one Spirit into one body -whether Jews or Greeks, slave or free- and we were all given the one Spirit to drink.
>
> Now the body is not made up of one part but of many. If the foot should say, 'Because I am not a hand, I do not belong to the body,' it would not for that reason cease to be part of the body. And if the ear should say, 'Because I am not an eye, I do not belong to the body,' it would not for that reason cease to be part of the body. If the whole body were an eye, where would the sense of hearing be? If the whole body were an ear, where

would the sense of smell be?..... As it is, there are many parts, but one body." (I Corinthians 12:12-17,20)

You could say it another way: "What good is an eye by itself?" NO GOOD! The Elevator Syndrome suffocates us like someone trapped in a garage with the car motor running. We know something stinks, and we are having a difficult time catching our breath, but we just don't see the magnitude of the problem yet.

Why be immersed in the Spirit of God? Why get out of the picture? If for no other reason than to break the Elevator Syndrome. It is only when we are one with Christ that we can break down the walls of separation and become one with each other. Jesus prayed, "Father, make them one as we are one."

Why? What's the point of our becoming one with others who are becoming one with the Spirit of God? What purpose does it serve? Other than the basic observation that we could finally move beyond racial, cultural, and socioeconomic barriers and truly be brother and sisters, what *are* some common sense reasons why God would intend for those who are connected to Him to be connected to each other?

SERVE GOD

If one of our primary purposes on this planet is to serve God's perfect will, doesn't it make sense that the more of us who are working *together* toward the fulfillment of that will, the more we will be able to accomplish for the glory of God? In other words, "Two heads are better than one."

Granted, all of us have been, and will be given, special gifts and be placed in individual situations which, for a time, will send us down a lonely road. But, if you look at the biblical example of being sent out in twos, our going at it alone is the exception. What we need to realize is that when we finally stop leaving evangelism up to the evangelism committees; missions up to the mission committees; faith-sharing up to the preacher; get away from saying, "That's not my job. I've done my share", and work together, great things are going to be done for the Kingdom of God!

SUPPORT AND STRENGTH

It is *through* our being united and connected that God provides **support and strength**.

"Fred" was in a similar boat to Allen, except that Fred was the one who was sick and suffering physically. I found out about Fred's illness about three months after he had recovered. I went by to see him one afternoon while I was out visiting. I had been in the house all of two minutes when he landed on me like the Marines on Iwo Jima! He raked me up and down about the hypocrisy of my church, about how they did not care for anyone else but themselves, and that they should not be able to call themselves Christians because no one had come to visit him during his time of need. For my part, I did not know Fred existed until the day before I went to see him. I guess that really is not an excuse. If I would have been a real Christian, I would have seen a vision of Fred calling to me in a dream to come to him. (Please note, there is a large degree of sarcasm in that last sentence.)

The situation for the church people was a little different. Most of the members of that little church *did* know Fred, and many of them had known him all of their lives.

I allowed Fred to vent his anger for about 30 minutes. He took a breath, looked me straight in the eye, and said, "So, what's your excuse?"

I said, "I don't have one. But I can explain where the people have been. Fred, you haven't darkened the door of that church in 20 years. You haven't kept in contact with the people of that church for at least that long. No one even knew you were sick in the first place. How would they have known to come and visit you?"

Needless to say, his response to that was not something I would feel comfortable putting in print. But his shortsightedness is a perfect example of the problem many of us have in our understanding of how God has designed His world and intends for it to work. Sure, God can, and often does, give strength and comfort to us when we are alone with Him. More often than not, however, God gives us that comfort and strength through others. By the same token, He is waiting *for us* to make ourselves available to Him so that we can be vessels He uses to give comfort and strength *to others*.

Keeping with Paul's image of the body, think of it this way: If you are an ear, how will you ever hear the soothing melody of beautiful music? Have you ever tried to turn on a radio with your ear. Try it. Make sure you video it. There could be some money in it if you submit it to one of those video programs. How will the ear ever hear the soothing music? The hand has to be obedient and help turn on the switch. But before the hand can turn the switch, the eye needs to get involved and help steer the hand to the proper location. Get the point? God has designed it so that we are together in order to be God's loving arms to a hurting world.

LAUGH

We need to laugh. One of the most ignored clichés of our day is "All work and no play makes Jack a dull boy." I would change that only slightly and say, "All work and no play... will kill you." At least it will kill your spirit. We need times to just kick our shoes off and laugh. We need these times to touch and inspire a part of our spirit that must be touched. Where else could we, or should we have greater joy than being *with*, and connected *to*, others who know the King of Joy?!

My all time favorite picture of Jesus is the one where Jesus' head is thrown back, tears are rolling down his cheeks, and he is about to bust a gut laughing. Whoever said Christians were always supposed to be serious and somber, did not know the Jesus I know. I never knew real joy and what it meant to laugh because of the joy deep within my heart until I came to know Jesus. In fact, I have said in every church I have ever served, "Christians are the strangest people I know." And we are strange precisely because of how we look at the world. We look at it through the eyes of Christ and in so doing find joy.

If misery loves company, laughter loves a crowd. Those who are being immersed in God are connected with others who are being immersed so that we can laugh!

GROWTH

It makes sense that we are connected to other believers because in, by, and through that connection we are helped to *grow* in our relationship with God. Think of it this way, if you want to be an artist, who should you hang around with? Artists! If you want to be an intellectual, who should you hang around with? Intellectuals! If you want to be a basketball player, where should you spend your time? Playing basketball with other basketball players. If you want to *be* a Christian, give your life to Jesus. If you want a helping hand in *being* Christian, hang out with other Christians.

People are never more obnoxious, judgmental, and conceited than when they are sitting in the comfort of their home, their feet up on the foot stool, a soft drink in one hand, the remote in the other, and yelling at the television about how dumb the players are, and "If it were up to me, I'd....." We seem to think we know it all when all we do is watch. When you are out on the field playing, you feel a lot less informed.

A few years ago, I was watching a North Carolina Tar Heel basketball game. About mid way through the game, North Carolina fell behind after Dean Smith made a wholesale substitution with what they used to call the "Blue team". In all of my wisdom and years of experience as a collegiate coach (which was nil), I turned to my wife and said, "You know, Dean's problem is that he keeps making too many substitutions." I had barely gotten those words out of my mouth, when the announcer remarked, "This will be Dean's 800th career victory."

We don't learn the game by sitting in the comfort of our homes casting out self-righteous judgments and wondering why everyone isn't as wonderful as we are. We learn only by getting in the game and working with others who are in the game.

I remember the first time I was asked to work with another group of ministers and volunteers on a conference level program. Though I couldn't see it then, I responded to those fellow Christians like I would if they were strangers on an elevator. I walked through the doors and had my mind set on getting to the top floor without any mishaps. Every once in awhile I would wonder what the others in the elevator might be thinking about me, but for the most part, I was simply watching the numbers go by until the project was done and it was time to head home. Needless to say, that first experience was not a real "humdinger" in my book. I think it would be safe to say that the others who *did* make some overtures of friendship to me through the weekend were also not all that impressed.

It was not until years later,.... you guessed it, when I started to discover what it meant to get out of the picture, that I began to break the elevator syndrome and start reaching out to others who had been reaching out to me. Guess what I found! Laughter! Friends! Others waiting to make my trip up and down much more enjoyable than I could have ever possibly imagined! Now, I even find myself looking forward to the ride.

One cool October morning, I stepped onto a half-full hospital elevator and pushed the button for the eleventh floor. By the second stop, the elevator was packed solid and creaking with every movement. I am sure even the atheists were praying. On the fourth stop, the doors opened to reveal seven nurses waiting to come on board. They looked in with pretty nurses' smiles and we looked out basically saying with our eyes, "You're not really going to get in here, are you?!" Sure enough, in they came! Everyone was smashed to the back of the elevator and the last nurse on had to use a shoe horn to make room. The door tried closing twice until we finally squeezed in enough for her to fit. That last nurse -now considered the anti-Christ by the majority of the elevator's passengers- had her back to the door looking into all of our angry eyes. She picked her head up a little, put a bright smile on her face and said, "I guess all of you are wondering why I called you here today."

It was amazing. What happened next was a phenomena! People laughed! In an elevator, people laughed. Then it became even more bizarre. People started talking with each other and sharing experiences relevant and not relevant to what was happening at the time. There was actual fellowship. By the time we reached the last floor, there was a sense of disappointment at the fact that we had to leave. I felt the strangest urge to make plans to ride again with everyone on the trip back down.

The elevator syndrome was broken!

What happens when we truly immerse ourselves in the Spirit of the living God? One more voice is heard. One more heart is touched. The parts start to come together as *one*.

CHAPTER 8

So that the world will be convinced!

"......so that the world may believe that you have sent me."
(John 17:21b   NIV)

For those who are astute observers, you will notice that this chapter starts with the same section of the Gospel of John used in the previous chapter. There Jesus' words were used to emphasize that a part of becoming immersed in the Spirit of God and getting out of the picture, is our becoming intricately connected to the rest of the Body of Christ. That chapter attempted to point out some of the common sense reasons God created us to be connected to everyone else who is connected to Him. However, that chapter left out *the* reason Jesus said God intended believers to be one. As the opening scripture of this chapter states, Jesus prayed that all Christians would be one *"so that* the world may believe that you have sent me." In essence, Jesus was saying that the unity of believers is one of *the* convincing proofs that Jesus Christ is who he said he was: King of kings, Lord of Lords, and Savior of the world.

I will go a step further. Only when Believers are immersed in the Spirit of God and get out of the picture will the world ever be *convinced* that Jesus is who we says he is.

Notice the wording used in that last sentence. It did not say that the world would be "intrigued", "made curious", or "interested". I said that only when those who call themselves Christians become immersed in the Spirit of God will the world ever be *convinced* that Jesus is all he says he is. Right now the world is not all that convinced. In fact, if they are convinced of anything, it is that this whole Christianity thing is a bunch of hog hooey. ("Hog Hooey" means "GARBAGE" for those of you who are not up on the latest intellectual vernacular.) Every time I talk with someone who is not a church-goer and/or not a Christian, I hear the same remarks: "Why should I bother with Jesus? He obviously hasn't made any difference in all of you."

"If church is all that great, why are there so much bickering and gossip going on?"

"Nah, the church has enough hypocrites."

"If God really is around, why is there so many wars.... *and*, why are a lot of those wars started by people who claim to be his followers?"

Somewhere I read a statement that put it best, "I would be more persuaded to believe that Jesus is who people say he is, if those who called on his name looked a little more saved."

A rabbi, in a debate with a prominent Christian theologian said this, "If Jesus is the Savior of the world, why doesn't the world look more saved?"

The answer to the rabbi's question is pretty simple: Those of us who call ourselves Christian are **still in the picture**! When Christians are still in the picture, all people see is *us*; our selfishness, our sins, our pride, our prejudices, our anger,.....us, and that is not very enticing. Believe me, the world needs convincing. **I** needed convincing.

I was raised in a minister's home. By all comparisons, my father was a great preacher, as well as a wonderful witness at home, for Jesus. There were, of course, the periodic times I believed my father was possessed by a demon. But what could I honestly expect when I had thrown a bicycle through our front window.

However, the reason my parents were not the convincing factor for me was because parents are supposed to be good witnesses. Likewise, preachers are *supposed* to talk about Jesus. Sure, what they said, and how they lived, got my attention, but I wasn't *convinced*. What I needed was some proof from my peers.

Though we had a huge youth group with many fine people, honestly speaking, bona fide, sold-out witnesses for Jesus were few and far between. We spent a great deal of time "relating" and discussing the finer points of moral and social issues, but we rarely got into what it meant to belong to Jesus hook, line, and sinker. I needed some proof from someone who had experienced a new life in Jesus. Religious clichés were fine for bumper stickers, but if I was going to commit my life to something, I wanted to be sure it was real.

One summer I went with my parents to a small camp in western New York state where my father was to speak. It was at this little Christian camp on a lake that I was finally convinced. I met four kids there who were learning what it meant to "get out of the picture." There was a difference in their lives! There was a light! In the midst of my darkness, I finally saw a faint glimmer at the end of the tunnel.

It was all I needed. I had heard the words, and was finally seeing those words become flesh. I was *convinced*. Jesus *was* more than something to talk about only on Sunday. Christianity went beyond just being religious and talking about a God you could not see. God *was* and *is* alive! His Spirit *did* and *does* change lives. I could see it in people just like me. All of it was real! I was convinced!

My need to be convinced, however, didn't stop with my initial salvation experience. Constantly, throughout my faith walk, whenever I have moved further into the arms of Jesus, it has almost always been after I have seen faith lived out through a fellow Christian; when I have been convinced that the words were real by a *living* example.

For example, I often *heard* about sharing my faith in Christ, but I never gave any of it a second thought until I *saw* witnessing exemplified in a friend of mine.

I *heard* about loving others, but never believed it was possible until I *saw* and experienced the love of other brothers and sisters.

I *heard* about the joy of knowing Christ, but I stayed on the fence until I *saw* what could only be described as the light of life in another Believer's eyes.

I heard.... I heard.... The world hears all the time. Never in the history of this planet has there been more access to the Good News of Jesus than today. Even the old communist block countries now have ample access to the Gospel of Christ. The problem is that everyone who has simply heard about the wonderful news of a perfect Savior now needs convincing that all the words are true. What the world needs now is exactly what it needed 2000 years ago. It needs all the words of God's love, faithfulness, patience, and power to become **real**... Flesh.

Two thousand years ago, the Word became flesh in Jesus Christ (John 1:1-5). All of who God was, is, and will forever be, took form in the person Jesus. At no other time has a man embodied the presence and Spirit of God as did that carpenter from Nazareth. Today, the world needs the same embodiment. In order for the world to be convinced, the world must again see the Word of God becoming flesh.

How's that for a tall order? Granted, we can't be another sacrifice for the world's sins. I know that our being filled with God's Spirit is not the same as Jesus being the incarnate word of God. But the fact still remains, what finally proved to a lost world that God's love was real and alive was when all the rhetoric became real and living. The point is that the world will remain lost unless we get out of the picture and allow it to see God in the flesh.... our flesh.

I guess the writer of the poem was right:

"Christ has not hands, but our hands to do His work today.
He has no feet, but our feet to guide men on His way.
He has no arms, but our arms to bring men to His side.
He has no tongue, but our tongues to tell men how He died.
We are the only Bible that the sinful world will read.
We are the sinner's gospel, we are the scoffer's creed.
We are the Lord's last message written in deed and word.
So what if the type is crooked or what if the print is blurred?"

Jesus made the point of this chapter pretty clear. First, he said, "**I** (Jesus) am the light of the world." (John 8:12) Later he said, "While I am in the world, I am the light of the world." (John 9:5) Then he alluded to the fact that the source of light here was going to change. He said to his followers, "*You* are the light of the world!" (Matthew 5:14) Finally, like a runner handing off the baton, he said to his followers, "'Peace be with you! As the father has sent me, I am sending you.' And with that he breathed on them and said, 'Receive the Holy Spirit.'" (John 20:21,22)

Why do we need to become immersed in God's Spirit? Why did God design it that we eventually be out of the picture? Because if we stay in the picture, when people look at us, that is exactly what they will see... *us*. If we are getting out of the picture, when people look at us, they will see the Spirit of God and say, "Hmmm, there might be something to this Jesus thing."

We need to get out of the picture in order to convince a lost world that Jesus is exactly who he said he was.

CHAPTER 9

Blessed Assurance

"The Spirit himself testifies with our spirit that we are God's children." (Romans 8:16 NIV)

A number of years ago, I was wallowing around in deep despair and doubt. I really did not know what to believe as far as God was concerned. Have you ever been there? Have you ever wondered, "Why did I fall for all of this religious stuff in the first place? None of this makes sense. Everyone I know thinks it's for losers. I don't know what to believe?"

Be honest. Have you ever asked yourself these questions? If not, I don't know whether to admire you or feel sorry for you. The reason I say that is because it has almost always been on the heels of my debilitating doubts that I have made the greatest strides into deeper faith. A wonderful Christian writer, William Barkley, put it best, "The person who works through his doubts to the belief that Jesus Christ is Lord, has attained a certainty that the person who unthinkingly accepts everything can never reach."

Whether you can relate to my struggle or not, suffice it to say that a number of years ago I was in bad shape. I clearly remember, on the eve of having to work at a large youth event in my conference, sitting in my living room crying to my wife, "I just don't know what to believe! If God is real, why doesn't He show Himself? What am I going to do?"

My wife is usually not at a loss for words. She almost always has some good insights into most situations. Not this time, however. She simply knelt by my side, held my hands, and said, "I don't know. Just be patient. You need some rest."

Ha! Rest was the last thing I was going to experience. The event at which I was scheduled to work promised an earth shattering eight to nine hours of total rest over a three day, jammed packed period. I don't know about you, but walking around in a semi-comatose state is hardly conducive for deep spiritual enlightenment.

As fate would have it, this event was designed to teach youth how to share their faith in Christ. Talk about hypocritical. I had about as much right being there as Hitler would have at a bar mitzvah.

It is no exaggeration to say that the majority of that weekend was only a blur. I remember bits and pieces here and there, but for the most part, I was numb and simply went through the motions. The only reason I was able to continue as a small group leader was that I kept hearing the words of a famous preacher, "Preach faith until you have faith." I figured that since I fit the "not have faith" section of that quote, if I kept preaching faith, I might again acquire faith. The bad news was that it wasn't working! If anything, by the middle of that weekend I was feeling even more faith*less*

The last night of the event was set aside for the youth to share stories about how Jesus had been real in their lives. As the time for that event was approaching, I thought that if there was ever going to be a time in which God would be able to get through to my darkened and doubting heart, it would be when a group of teens talked about how real God was in their lives. BUT, alas, even during what was evidently a moving service for everyone else, all that came to my mind was, "What a crock! These kids have been duped too! I've been sitting here for hours. I wonder if anyone would notice if I left."

The next morning I woke up with some real apprehension. I knew that if I had missed the Spirit's movement the night before, my relationship with God must really be in bad shape. I continued to go through the required motions of the morning, dreading every minute that brought me closer to the closing worship service. The emphasis of the closing worship was Pentecost, and as a part of the service we would be taking part in the Lord's Supper. The last thing I wanted to do was hear more about the Holy Spirit -an **unseen** force- and be forced to leave my seat to take part in a ritual. Needless to say, I was really a pathetic mess.

What made matters worse was where they placed the leaders. I was not going to be able to get lost in the crowd or hide in the back. In order for the leaders to quickly move into place for the Lord's Supper, we were seated *up front*.

There I sat, doing my best to look as dejected, and bored as I possibly could. I managed to maintain my disapproving scowl through most of the service and into the closing minutes. But, then it happened. Yes, the Spirit started to move in me.

One of the other leaders at this event was a very gifted singer and pianist. He felt a "nudging from God", as he put it, to lead the group in one last song. Picking up his guitar, and pulling the bow back holding the arrow aimed at my heart, he started singing the old Gospel song, "Soon & Very Soon." The words of the opening verse are: "Soon and very soon, we are going to *see* the King. Soon and very soon, we are going to *see* the King. Soon and very soon, we are going to *see* the King. Hallelujah, hallelujah, we're going to *see* the King."

I couldn't believe it! Of all the songs... of all the words that I did not want to sing, it was a song about "*seeing*" God. Though seeing God was exactly what I wanted to do, I did not want to be disappointed again. Over the weeks prior to that event I had hoped beyond hope that God would reveal Himself in some miraculous and unquestionable way. Nothing. But, as I stood there singing that old hymn, I heard what was as close to an audible voice as I have ever heard. In the midst of 150 plus youth and adults singing at the top of their lungs I heard, "Jim, do you want to see Me? Turn around."

In my mind I asked, "What? Do what?"

The voice again said, "Turn around."

I did. I turned around,...... and I saw God. I did not see a floating mist or some Hollywood special effect. I saw the face of God in the faces of the people behind me. Then, as clearly as I had heard The Voice seconds before, I heard, "See, I am here. Look, and believe."

The feeling I experienced at that time can not be adequately described. All I can plainly say is that I was **assured**! God let me know in no uncertain terms that He **IS**!

I am thrilled to say, that though I have periodically experienced some "dark nights of the soul" from time to time, God has continued to make available to me that same assurance He gave me that wondrous Sunday morning.

Let me clarify something though. My continuing sense of assurance has not been based solely on that one particular experience. Every once in awhile we all need a special boost from the Lord. The good news is that He meets us at our point of need. The reason I have not lost that assurance, the reason I have not crashed into the particular depths of that debilitating doubt again, is because the experience at that youth training event took place about the same time I began to experience what it means to be immersed in God. The point is; if I had to rely on extra ordinary, spiritual experiences to maintain my faithful confidence, I would be in sorry shape. My assurance *now* comes because, as Paul so beautifully put it, "The Spirit himself testifies with my spirit that I am a child of God." (Romans 8:16)

What makes the assurance so readily available now as compared to before, is that as I continue to work toward there being less of me and more of Him, I can hear God's assuring voice much better and more frequently.

Why did God intend for us to be out of the picture, to be immersed in the Spirit of God? Because when we finally get off the fence and commit fully to Him, we can experience the assuring Truth we so desperately need to remain bold, faithful disciples of Christ.

CHAPTER 10

Looking Through Clearer Glass

"Now we see but a poor reflection as in a mirror; then we shall see face to face." (I Corinthians 13:12   NIV)

Do you recognize this scripture?   It is from the thirteenth chapter of first Corinthians, otherwise known as "The Love Chapter". It is in the love chapter that Paul talks about "the most excellent way".....love. After describing in chapter 12 of I Corinthians the wonderful gifts the Holy Spirit has waiting for those who make themselves available to his in-filling, Paul puts everything in perspective in chapter 13 by saying, in essence, "All of these gifts are fine and good, but demonstrating *any* of these gifts without love is worthless!"

Here it is in black and white:

"If I speak in the tongues of men and of angels, but have not love, I am only a resounding gong or a clanging cymbal. If I have the gift of prophecy and can fathom all mysteries and all knowledge, and if I have a faith that can move mountains, but have not love, I am nothing." (I Corinthians 13:1,2)

Gets right to the point, doesn't he? I will try to do the same. Only when we begin to get out of the picture and become immersed in the Spirit of God will we *ever* be able to see God's world and all that is in it the way He sees it and, in so doing, learn how to love it. Paul gave a wonderful analogy: as long as we remain in the picture, we are going to be seeing through a poor reflection in a mirror. The King James Version makes the point even more descriptive. It says, "For now we see through a glass darkly." In other words, the picture *we* see of the world -left to the input of mortal eyes- is fuzzy, dirty, and smeared. And the picture is that way because of our prejudices, ignorance, fears, disappointments, insecurities, and self-centeredness. Only *in* God will we be able to see clearly and, in so doing, love fully.

I am not sure if my father originated this phrase or "borrowed" it from another minister and I missed the footnote someplace, but my father used to call the source of our blurred vision, "navel gazing". Navel gazing is essentially what it sounds like: gazing at one's navel.

Let me clarify here. Navel gazing has nothing to do with sitting on a beach and watching uncovered navels parade up and down the shore line. Navel gazing is when our attention and focus is turned solely inward on ourselves. It goes without saying -though I'm saying it anyway- that it's hard to see clearly when we navel gaze. Try this experiment: Pull your shirt up so that you can see your belly button. Now, lean over as far as you can and stare intently at your navel. Keep staring for at least 30 seconds. Don't cheat! This experiment won't work if you cheat. In fact, make it one full minute to make up for all of those who are cheating right now. After 30 to 60 seconds of intently staring at your navel, jerk your head up quickly and look at an object somewhere around you. Having trouble focusing? Things a little blurred? That is because everything is blurred when we spend the majority of our time looking inward. Only when we spend time looking outward, can things apart from us come into clear focus. *And,* only when we are immersed in God's Spirit are we really ever going to *be able* to look outward, and slowly move away from our natural tendency to navel gaze.

What are the benefits of being a non-navel gazer,.... other than the fact that you won't be running into walls quite as often?

SEE OTHERS CLEARLY

First of all, we will begin to see others as God sees them. No longer will our perception of reality be clouded by our own self-centered jealousies and insecurities; i.e. "How is everything affecting me?" Rather, we will be given *open* eyes to see others as God sees them, in all of their wonder, glory, failures, value.... and truly begin to love and appreciate them as God does: **Unconditionally**.

A marvelous example of someone who looked at others through more loving, and appreciative eyes than his own was Abraham Lincoln. When he was elected president of the United States, Stanton said of him, "Lincoln is a cunning clown," and he nicknamed Lincoln "the original gorilla." In response to this disrespectful insult, Lincoln made Stanton his minister of war and patiently and courteously worked with him over the years.

Did it have an effect on Stanton? Yes! The night Lincoln was shot, Stanton was standing by Lincoln's death bed, and through tear-filled eyes said of Lincoln, "There lies the greatest ruler of men the world has ever known." If not for Lincoln's ability to "get himself out of the picture" and begin seeing through clearer glass, Stanton would have remained a hard, prejudiced, angry man.

If we can move beyond navel-gazing, we will begin to know the joy of loving others unconditionally, as God loves.

ETERNAL PERSPECTIVE

The second benefit of being a non-navel gazer and seeing the world as God sees it, is that we can begin to acquire an *eternal perspective*.

Corey Ten Boone, the author of "The Hiding Place", when others were getting carried away over inconsequential matters, often asked, "Is it eternal?" *That* is an excellent question. It is a question, however, that we really cannot grasp until we begin to see through God's eyes.

Before we grow into a deeper perspective, we see every situation like a teenager would see it. What I mean by that is, teens are notorious for making a mountain out of a mole hill. If there is a pimple on the nose, it spells certain death for half of the world's population. If the favorite jeans are not clean when one is getting ready for school, then there really is no use in going to school because life is now a total loss. You get the point. For those of you who have teens, you are probably smiling a knowing smile. We would love to attribute all oversensitivity and irrational behavior to high hormonal persons between the ages of 10 and 20, but it just isn't so. If the shoe fits -and it does- we need to wear it. Everyone, adults included, find it very difficult to put what is happening to us at any given moment in its proper "eternal" perspective.

For example, while I was serving a small country church in Georgia, I decided to take the afternoon and visit some of my congregation who lived in the area. The first sign that this particular afternoon was not going to go well was that the climate was very hot and sticky. What made matters worse was that I was running late for my visits *and* I had misplaced my car keys. I am usually somewhat compulsive about putting my keys in the same location so that I won't have to waste any time trying to round them up. But, somehow, (I know it was a plot of Satan), I had lost my keys.

I will have to brag on myself for just a few lines. The first 10 minutes or so, I searched the house in a very relaxed manner. I went through every room giving it a good, general "once over." I even remember patting myself on the back for how well I was controlling myself in the midst of this earth shattering disaster. The house of cards began to fall, though, when time began running out and my keys were nowhere to be found.

I need to point out here that I had only completed the "quick run through" method of searching a house for something. The next inevitable step was to move into the "meticulous search" mode.

"What is the meticulous search mode?" you ask

Good question. The "meticulous search mode" is when a person starts in one corner of the house and searches everywhere he or she can possibly search, regardless of how ridiculous it might be to search there. The object is to stay calm and to be thorough. I was doing pretty good with the "thorough". I was having a little trouble with the "calm".

For those of you who have been through this process, you know the next step. I quickly moved into the "grab and slam" stage of searching. The name pretty much speaks for itself. Basically, you run through the house, yelling at the top of your lungs, spitting saliva on the floor, and grabbing everything you can reach -pretending to *still* be looking for the object- and slamming it down with all of your might in a vain attempt to scare the object into revealing itself. I was in the midst of a rather *loud* version of "grab and slam" when I finally made my way into the bathroom. I opened up the lid to the "John" and then slammed it down so hard that I split the seat in half.

You are probably wondering two things at this point: 1) Why was I looking in the bathroom, and specifically *inside* the "john"? Like I said, I was trying to be thorough. 2) How in the world can you break a toilet seat in half? I guess that just goes to show you how upset -not to mention immature- I was.

After 30 minutes of ranting and raving through the house, my keys were still nowhere in sight. So, I decided to run over to the church -which was about 30 feet from the parsonage (trailer)- and see if I could find them there. As I was walking toward the church, I noticed that someone had left the basement door open. This just added to my already warped conviction that someone was out to get me and that this diabolical group was probably the same people who took part in the assassination of J.F.K. I walked into the basement, slammed the door shut, spun around, and found myself staring into the eyes of one of the most saintly women God ever put on this earth.

Oh! Did I tell you the parsonage windows *and* the church windows had been open during my entire tirade?

Yep! She heard it all. Everything down to the splitting of the toilet seat. She smiled and asked, "Wellllll, how are we today?"

She might have been fine. I was about to die!

There was a great deal of sarcasm in her voice. Not only was she a saint, but she had a wonderful sense of humor. I know for a fact that in that instance that saintly woman saw what had unparalleled potential for being a huge joke to hold over the minister's head for years to come. I wish I could remember what I said to her. The only thing I know for sure is that I got sick to my stomach and wanted to crawl in the nearest hole. It did not have to be a very big hole either. She and I both knew how small and shallow I was being at that moment.

Have you ever been there? Sure you have. We all have. Do you want to leave it behind? You can. We can. How? Get out of the picture. Immerse yourself in God, as He intended, so that you can see through eyes that clearly show what matters.

I think Amy Grant's song, "Father's Eyes," expresses what my prayer is for me.... for you; and what is possible:

"I may not be every mother's dream for her little girl. My face may not grace the mind of everyone in the world. But that's all right, as long as I can have one wish I pray, when people look inside my life, I want to hear them say, 'She's got her Father's eyes. Eyes that find the good in things, when good is not around. Eyes that find the source of help when help just can't be found. Eyes full of compassion, seeing every pain, knowing what you're going through and feeling it the same. Just like her Father's eyes. ("Father's Eyes" by Amy Grant)

Since I just dealt with the idea of obtaining perspective, I have to put in this one last example of seeing things clearly. I am putting it in for no other reason than it says it so clearly, and I get a big kick out of it when I read it. I first found it in Charles Swindoll's book "Seasons of Life". Here it is. A letter from a young lady off at school to her mom and dad:

"Dear Mom and Dad,

I just thought I'd drop you a note to clue you in on my plans. I've fallen in love with a guy named Jim. He quit high school after grade 11 to get married. About a year ago he got a divorce.

We've been going steady for two months and plan to get married in the fall. Until then, I've decided to move into his apartment -I think I might be pregnant.

At any rate, I dropped out of school last week, although I'd like to finish college sometime in the future.

Mom and Dad, I just want you to know that everything I've written so far in this letter is false. *None* of it is true.

But Mom and Dad, it *is* true that I got a "C" in French and flunked math. It *is* true that I'm going to need some money for my tuition payments.

Your loving daughter,"

Now *that's* perspective on things. The destination God has in store for us is to acquire His perspective by being immersed in His Spirit.

CHAPTER 11

Following the hash marks down the trail

"Trust in the Lord with all your heart and lean not on your own understanding; in all your ways acknowledge him, and he will make your paths straight." (Proverbs 3:5,6 NIV)

A number of years ago, I was out on a family backpacking trip with some people from my church. We started on a weekend jaunt through the woods on Friday and ended at a beautiful camp site tucked back in a forest next to a gorgeous meadow called "Old Orchard". Once we stumbled into Old Orchard, we did the usual backpacking activities of resting our weary legs, sitting around, and talking about why we were willing to strap 40 pounds on our backs and go meandering through the jungles of the deep Appalachian Mountains, and who had the biggest blisters. Tough, manly stuff like that.

Being my regularly compulsive, yet charmingly responsible self, I did not feel comfortable missing a Sunday from the pulpit in order to go gallivanting around in the woods with a bunch of demented backpackers. In order to avoid missing a Sunday, I decided to head back early Sunday morning so that I could bless my congregation with a wonderfully earth-moving sermon delivered by a bone-tired minister. The difficult thing about going back early was that I was going to have to wake up at around 5:30 AM to give myself time to hike out from camp, make it down to the road, and then drive the two and a half hour trip back home.

Oh! Did I tell you that we were about two miles back in the woods? Did I also tell you that this was a *fall* hike? Here is the million dollar question: "What happens in the fall?" That's right! You guessed it! The leaves *fall*. What generally happens when the leaves fall in the deep woods? For those of you who are not from the country, the leaves usually cover the ground. They cover the ground to the point you need a hound dog to find dirt.

Now, please allow me one more question to help set the proper mood for this story: "Where was I?" The answer: Two miles away from any path larger than a pig crossing, back in the deep woods, faced with the "opportunity" of walking a narrow, winding, leaf covered trail at 5:30 in the morning, by myself.... and it was dark. Do you remember what was said earlier about the size of flashlights backpackers take? To refresh your memory, suffice it to say that you could use one of these flashlights as a tooth pick. It was under these marvelous circumstances that I set out on my heroic pilgrimage to share the Good News with my "eager" flock.

All of these wonderful aspects did not really occur to me until I was about 25 yards away from the camp. What finally helped this exciting situation sink into my razor sharp mind was the fact that when I reached the edge of the clearing, the path disappeared under a blanket of multicolored leaves. There was, of course, the option of turning back. The simple reason I did not turn back was pride. That's right, pure, unadulterated pride. How would it look if the group leader had to walk back to the tents and ask someone to walk him down to his car? In retrospect, had I asked for help in getting down to my car, it would have looked like the leader had a few brains in his head. Alas, I did not. Contrary to my better judgment -not to mention my shaking knees- I set off down the trail.

Needless to say, I wondered off the trail a time or two. There were places where the trail was semi-clear, and then right around a sharp bend, the trail would completely disappear under a blanket of leaves. Whenever the trail disappeared, I would take a few more steps into the unknown, freeze in sheer terror.... and pray! Boy howdy, would I pray!

"How did I make it out?" you ask. It seems that the wise and all knowing people who designed the Appalachian trail possessed unique insight into the poor pathetic people who would later walk those hallowed ways. They decided that if, by some chance, there was some fool, idiotic enough to walk a leaf covered trail in the middle of the night, they were going to give him something else to find his way out. So, they had some saintly volunteers place white hash marks along the path about every 50 yards or so. Once I regained my composure, stopped hyperventilating, and remembered the hash marks, getting out was not all that bad.

Keep in mind, the darkness did not disappear. I was not instantaneously teleported to my vehicle. I was still in the dark, and I was still a good two miles away from my destination. The key was that I now knew the markers would direct my path. And I knew I was going to be able to make my way out *if* I took my time to follow them.

Every time I ventured from the path, I would stop and sweep the woods with my toothpick size flashlight. Sooner or later -and I was constantly requesting of God that He would make it *sooner*- I would spot a hash mark on a distant tree or rock. I would walk to the hash mark and if the trail was visible, would walk on until I lost my way. I would once again remain still until I spotted the next hash mark and then move on. That was the way I made it all the way down that mountain.

What is the point? Simple: "Trust in the Lord with all your heart. Lean not on your own understanding. In all your ways acknowledge Him, and he will make your paths straight." (Proverbs 3:5,6 NIV) Does this scripture remind you of anything? Possibly words like, "If anyone would find his life, he must lose it." or "God's desire is that we are out of the picture." might ring a bell. The writer of this Proverb is saying exactly what this book has been saying from the "get-go": Get out of God's way and some pretty "nifty" things could happen. The "nifty" thing this proverb is referring to is *guidance*; specifically, *God's* guidance, *God's* direction.

Guidance!

The point I am making is that we *can* know the path. We *can* make the right choices. We *can* stay on the right road. We *can* make it to our destination, *if* we rely on God's guidance. And, we can only really begin to know and experience God's guidance when we start getting out of the picture and allowing God to lead.

Think of it this way; there is a group of caring people called the Appalachian Trail Committee who went to all the trouble to paint rocks and trees, and put up clearly marked signs for people they were never going to meet. How likely, if God is who He says He is, is our loving heavenly Father going to make sure the right signs are marking the right paths for His children? Much more likely!

Read the scripture again, "Trust in the Lord with all your heart. Lean not on your own understanding. In all your ways acknowledge Him, and He will make your paths straight." (Proverbs 3:5,6)

How then do we experience His guidance.

RECOGNIZE THE VOICE

The first thing that comes to mind is: Learn to recognize God's Voice.

Have you noticed how a child can hear her mother's voice in a crowded room? Have you ever noticed how a parent can hear his child despite the presence of the loudest racket? Have you ever been some place in a throng of people and heard your name called out by your "sweety" and have known exactly who it was? All of these are possible because we have learned to recognize the person's voice.

A few years ago, I was at a school carnival with my daughters. Actually, they were already there and I was supposed to find them among the thousand or so who were present. I walked around for about 15 minutes wondering how in the world I was going to find my two kids in the middle of all of these other runny nosed, "I want more money" youngins running around loose. Just as I was about to lose hope, I heard from about 25 feet behind me, "Daddy!"

Keep in mind, I was hardly the only "Daddy" in the area. I would venture to guess that there were at least 50 other daddies in my immediate area. That fact made absolutely no difference. When I heard this particular "Daddy!", I turned around immediately because I recognized the voice. More to the point, no other "daddy" did. It was my youngest daughter. How did I know it was my child? Simple: There was a connection between us, I had spent time with her, and I recognized her voice.

Do you want to be able to hear the voice of God leading you down the path? Then stay connected, spend time with Him, and you will learn to recognize His voice.

I have found, as I have been more immersed in the presence of God, that I can recognize His voice better. I can hear His voice in the middle of a din saying, "This is the direction you need to go." I can hear His voice say to my heart, "Here are the words you are groping for." I can hear his voice in the quiet moments saying, "Rest, and know that I am God."

God does not always speak in full sentences though. There are times when God's voice is simply a powerful, "GO!" or "STOP!"

Good examples of God speaking in powerful, one word impulses, and in full sentences are two situations I regularly face in my ministry. When I am writing a sermon, preparing a devotion, and most definitely sitting down to work on this book, I am listening to God's small voice. Ninety percent of what is in this book is dictation. The remaining ten percent -the bad stuff- is something we just could never completely edit out. But no matter what I am working on, God is speaking full sentences, complete thoughts, and unique insights. At least they are unique to me at the time.

On the other hand, I could be driving down the road and feel the sudden impulse to stop at a particular house. Or, I could be sitting in my study working on something, and a name of someone in my church would come blasting into my mind from out of nowhere. At first I used to ignore the "blasting in" of names. I ignored them until I began to see a pattern forming. I ignored them until I realized that almost every time a person's name came to mind, it was at a time that he or she was going through something in which I should have been available. It was not until I began to recognize and acknowledge that "impulse" that I began to do the ministry God had in mind for me to do instead of what I had on my agenda for that day.

During the writing process of this book, I was up early one morning running an errand, and had the strong impulse to stop and visit one of the shut-ins in the church. Because of my plans to work on this book, however, I decided I would wait until the next day to go by and see her. When I checked my answering machine at the office before I headed out to my study, there was a message from that person's home-health nurse letting me know that she had just taken a turn for the worse. I changed my schedule for that day.

God is waiting to guide our paths. Our pure joy is spending enough time with Him and becoming so immersed in Him that we can begin to recognize His voice.

OTHERS

If we are in the process of getting out of the picture and being immersed in the Spirit of God, we can experience God's guidance by recognizing His voice and His impulse speaking to our inner spirits. But hearing God's direction is not relegated to only an individual's inner spiritual ear. God also guides us -if we listen- through our Christian brothers and sisters. In other words, you can write a friend of mine a thank you note, or even a "thanks a lot" note, because if it was not for him, you would not be holding this book in your hands today.

When I was beginning to feel a real leading from God that I should write this book, my initial reaction was, "You've got to be kidding! I have too much to do. And besides, who am I that I should write a book?"

After a few months of dealing with this burden, I mentioned it to a friend of mine. He said, "Hmmm."

He is a very deep fellow.

About a week went by and I found myself in a small group discussion with this particular friend and a few others from my church. The discussion topic was: "What is God calling you to do?" Two of us in the group were clearly feeling God's leading to write, but we were both reluctant for a variety of reasons. After we finished our litany of whining and excuses, my friend said, "Anybody who knows God's will and doesn't do it is an idiot."

It wasn't anything earth-shattering or philosophical, but through those few words God said to me, "Yeah! Listen to what he's telling you. I want you to do this!"

A few years ago I would not have been able to hear, much less accept my friend's remarks. I would have been too insulted to hear what he was trying to say. It wasn't until..... Hmmm... Let me think. When was it? Oh yes! Now I remember. It was when I began to be immersed in God's Spirit and to get out of the picture that I began to realize how I am connected to the rest of the body, and that God could work through that body *if* I would shut-up and listen.

To say it another way, once we begin to get out of the picture, not only can we begin to hear God's voice in our own heart, speaking softly to our own soul, but we can begin to recognize His voice speaking through *others*, through books, remarks, sermons, and conversations.

OPENED DOORS

Lastly, we can experience God's guidance through what I have always referred to as "opened and closed doors". A good biblical illustration of this is the account of Paul's ministry in the sixteenth chapter of the book of Acts. The account reads as follows:

> "Paul and his companions traveled throughout the region of Phyrgia and Galatia, having been kept by the Holy Spirit from preaching the word in the providence of Asia. When they came to the border of Mysia, they tried to enter Bithynia, but the Spirit of Jesus would not allow them to." (Acts 16:6 & 7)

"....but the Spirit of Jesus would not allow them to." I wonder how the Spirit of Jesus did not allow them. Maybe things just "did not work out" for them to go into Asia. In other words, because Paul and his cohorts could not, or would not hear God's voice telling them not to go, God orchestrated events which would be a semi-clear road block telling them to turn around and go the other way.

It's possible. I have experienced it a number of times. I have usually experienced God opening and closing doors when, because of my own inability to separate my emotions from a decision, I have been unable to clearly hear His voice.

Marriage is a good example. When I attended my small Christian, Liberal Arts college, *the* line used to pick up girls was, "It's God's will that we go out." Or "I feel it's God's will that we get married eventually." In fact, my wife was fed that line at least a half dozen times before she had the good fortune to meet me. My line was, "I'm broke. We're going Dutch." I clearly remember the struggle I had in truly knowing if *this* particular woman was the one God wanted me to walk the trail with for the rest of my life. Think of all the emotions running rampant during the dating years. Of course a young, hormone driven boy is going to think that the girl he is madly in love with is the one God wants him to marry. Certainly God wants me with the girl who sends me into a quiver at the slightest touch. At least it is a certainty until we get into a huge fight, break up, and I find another young lass who has the same effect on me.

How *do* you know? I remember praying, "God, make it possible or block the road. I'm too confused to hear you clearly." The point is, God was faithful to answer that prayer, but we fail to recognize that answer until we get out of the picture and start the process of becoming immersed in His Spirit.

Guidance! What does it look like to become immersed in God's Spirit; to get out of the picture? We are able to hear God's voice, walk His path, and reach "the car."

CHAPTER 12

Leaving The Wine Press

"Jesus answered.... 'If you love me, you will obey what I command.'" (John 14:15)

The country was under siege. Every able-bodied man was doing everything he could to keep the approaching army at bay. Everybody except our hero. While the enemy was pillaging and looting the countryside, our hero was hiding in the wine press threshing out some grain. You can call it whatever you want. Call our hero a coward, or call him smart. Either way, where we find him is hiding in the dark, trying to eke out a few grains in order to make a loaf of bread or two. Then, out of nowhere, God calls. God says to our hero, "Hero, I want you to go and defeat the army that is destroying this land."

Can you imagine our hero's response? "What?! Who me?! I am nobody. My family is nothing. In fact, if you line up all the families of our nation, mine is the least important, and I am the least important in my family. In other words, God, I think you have the wrong number."

God responds, "Nope! Sorry. You're the guy I've been looking for." I would assume God was looking for this particular guy because *if* the battle was won, only God would be worthy of the praise. *This* clodhopper was anything but a military genius.

To make a long story short, after a few tests by our hero to make sure God was indeed calling him to fight the battle, our hero gives in and calls the people together.

Do you recognize the story? It's the story of Gideon. What is the story of Gideon doing in a chapter on obedience? Gideon was not a person spectacularly endowed with the gift of faithfulness. If anything, God took Gideon kicking and screaming into battle. The reason Gideon is mentioned here, is to show how Gideon sifted through the "volunteers" to put together his army.

According to the seventh chapter of the book of Judges, God had a unique way of sifting out those who would be sent into battle against the opposing army. First of all, God told Gideon that in order to ensure that God would get the praise for the victory over the Midianite army, Gideon was to tell the thirty-two thousand who showed up to fight that if any of them had any fear, they could go home. Twenty two thousand took Gideon up on his offer and went home. You can almost see Gideon running behind them saying, "No, wait! Maybe if you're only *real* scared. If you're just kind of frightened, stick around!"

Gideon was left with only ten thousand to fight more than one hundred thousand. The ten thousand who remained were still too many to ensure that God would get the glory. God told Gideon to take the ten thousand to the top of a hill and get them ready for battle. God's instructions were to watch the men as they made their way down the hill and passed by a place to drink. Those who drank like a dog and kept moving were to stay with Gideon and those who took off their equipment to get a good filling were to be sent home. Here's the bad news. Only three hundred lapped the water like a dog. So, there was Gideon, standing with his three hundred dog lappers, watching the remaining nine thousand and seven hundred go home. I would imagine that if Gideon was not apprehensive up to that point, he was now!

God wanted men who were going to be faithful. God knew He could use men in a miraculous way who were sold out in their obedience to Him. But why gauge someone's faithfulness on how they drink water? Simple, those who drank like dogs had their minds on one thing: The battle. They were not interested in quenching any selfish thirst. They had been given a burden from the Lord, and fulfilling their commission was all that mattered.

The story of Gideon sifting his army down to the truly faithful reminds me of when my father lived in Georgia. He was roped into going coon hunting with one of the men in his church. One of the reasons my father agreed to go, even with his ridiculously busy schedule, was that he wanted to see this man's dogs in action. Throughout the entire county, this man's hounds were famous. They had won hunting trophy after hunting trophy and brought top dollar as dogs for breeding. My father wanted to see for himself these fabulous dogs in action.

As they started the hunt, he didn't notice anything unusual about the dogs compared to the other dogs hunting with them that day. They all made the same noises. They all ran as one large pack. They all seemed to be following the same scent. It wasn't until they had been hunting for a few hours and the dogs were getting tired, that the difference began to stand out. The separating moment in the hunt was when the pack hit a large creek deep in the woods. After hunting for most of the morning on what was a relatively hot day, once the pack hit the water, the hunters ground to a halt because the vast majority of the pack decided to take a break.

My father said it was a sight to behold. There were all of these husky Georgia farmers standing on the side of a creek, watching their top dollar hounds roll around in the water and mud like a bunch of kids just let out for summer vacation. In many ways, the hounds were making such a fuss that the owners were getting a little embarrassed. All of them except,.... you guessed it, the man who invited my father. His dogs were nowhere to be found. Why? They did not stop to play around. They had been commanded by their owner, had a mission to carry out, and they shot through that water, lapped as they went, kept their eyes on the goal, and never missed a beat.

Guess who got the coon!

Dogs catching their prey, soldiers ready for battle, take your pick. All of them speak of what becomes *natural* for the

Christian who is immersed in the Spirit of God: ***Obedience***. Obedience. That ability to see the hash marks on the trail and to walk in that direction!

The best Biblical example of this some guy praying in a garden. This guy knew that he had been called to accomplish a terrible task. He knew that he would suffer pain, rejection, misunderstanding, and betrayal. He even knew that in the midst of his pain, God would seem to be distant and aloof. He was not thrilled about what lay ahead of him. He was not jumping for joy over the fact that God had called him to suffer. Yet, he still prayed, "Not my will but Thine."

The guy's name was Jesus. The example he set is what he expects us to follow. It may not be what we would choose were we to write the script. It may not be the most pleasant experience in the world. But for those who are getting out of the picture, there really is no choice. Prior to any specific call to battle, the choice has already been made; "Not my will, but Thine, O Lord!"

Notice what Jesus says in the opening scripture of this chapter. He does not say, "If you obey me, I will love you." *That* is the interpretation many of us have heard and even perpetuate by saying it to others. Our obedience has nothing to do with making God love us. Rather, our obedience has everything to do with *demonstrating* our love for God.

Think of it this way. What happens when you fill a person up with whiskey? Basically they act stupid. If you are a big whiskey drinker, the only reason your friends do not tell you how dumb you act when you get drunk is because they enjoy laughing at you.

When someone fills himself with whiskey, he cannot help but act stupid. That is the nature of the drink. It dulls your senses, clouds your mind, and impairs your judgment. In other words, it compels you to do things you would not otherwise do.

Though the analogy lacks a few points, the same is true for another type of Spirit. When one is filled with the Spirit of

God, one is compelled to act in accordance with the nature of that Spirit. If people have a problem jumping up on a table and making a fool out of themselves, then they take a little swig and before they know it, they're up on the oak wood dancing the watoosy. If I have a hard time standing up to boldly proclaim the Gospel of Jesus, if I work toward immersing myself in the Spirit of God, before I know it, I will be kneeling down in a living room helping another lost soul find his way home.

We, by nature, are creatures who are controlled by the spirit which fills us. When we are filled with God's Spirit, we are *naturally* obedient to His call.

Don't miss that word "naturally." Over and over again I have heard from Christians who are seeking to be more obedient that *they* are not able to do all that they feel is expected of them. They tell me that *they* can't be loving enough, forgiving enough, or nice enough. They can concentrate real hard and for a time be good little Christian boys and girls, but eventually they invariably slip up because *they* just don't have the strength to keep going.

That's right! *We* don't have the strength to be permanently good on our own. Christian moral living is not a matter of pulling yourself up by your bootstraps and making yourself good enough. Christian moral living comes when we die to self and are so filled with the Spirit of God that God and His goodness flow out of us **naturally**.

Well then, if God is waiting for us to have His Spirit flow through us and enable us to be obedient, what then makes obedience so difficult? Other than our *not* being immersed in God's Spirit, why are we almost always having to be dragged into the battle? I can think of a few reasons.

God is slow

First of all, I struggle with obedience because of how slow God is in following up.

I have often thought that I would probably be more faithful if the results of my faithfulness were more immediate. Like Jesus, I might be able to give all of me, if in *three days* the results would come through. But how often does God act in three days? Not very often. In fact, I would say almost never. As someone once said, "God's time is not our time." You better believe it. If God were a business person in this day and age, He would have gone bankrupt years ago. Nobody frequents an establishment which promises something and then keeps the customer hanging. We want it yesterday, not "whenever the time is right."

Not only are the results of our obedience delayed, but God tends to take His sweet time in letting us know how He wants us to obey to in the first place. What I mean is, we could be standing at one of those hash marks on the trail for years, knowing God has a direction for us, but He's just not ready to let us know for sure what that direction is or where that next hash mark lies.

So, we have trouble being obedient because God is not a TV dinner.

Difficult tasks

The second reason we have trouble being faithful is because of the difficulty of the tasks God calls us to do.

Take a look at Gideon. Here he is with only three hundred men and called into battle against over one hundred thousand. If it were me, I would chock the whole "God called me" thing up to indigestion and go back to threshing wheat in the wine press before I got into too much trouble. God does indeed call us to do some very difficult tasks.

Just imagine Christ's last order to his followers: "Go and make disciples of all nations..." (Matthew 28:19a) I would assume they felt a little overwhelmed at the time. No wonder Peter decided to take the whole bunch fishing. Catching a few carp would be considerably easier than changing the heart of a sick world.

What others think of us

Thirdly, what often makes obedience to God the most difficult is the fear of what others might think about us because of some of the strange things God asks us to do.

Take a look at Gideon again. According to the account in Judges, God instructs Gideon to gather the men together and arm them primarily with torches, bowls, and trumpets. I can just hear Gideon giving the instructions to his men.

"Okay fellas. Here's the plan. Some of you take the bowls, some of you take the torches, and the rest of you take the trumpets."

"What are we going to do with these, boss?" some confused soldier asks.

"Well, we're going to surround the Midianites, sound our trumpets, break our jars, hold up our torches and yell, 'A sword for the Lord and for Gideon!' That should really scare these highly trained soldiers, and they should turn on themselves and kill one another." Can you see most of the men looking at each other with an "I wonder what he has been smoking" look?

The man next to Gideon says, "Uhhhh, yeah! Come over here Gideon and lie down. You'll feel better in the morning."

But *that* is exactly what God had told Gideon to do. Not quite the conventional battle plan of that day... or *any* day for that matter. If the men under his command did not laugh, it was a good bet the people who were asked to provide the "weapons did. Sometimes the worst part of being obedient to God is the ridicule or misunderstanding we receive from others who just do not understand.

Abraham's family probably did not understand why he went off following some voice he believed to be of The one true God.

David's brothers thought he was a nut when he went out to fight Goliath.

I don't think one of the prophets ever avoided being thought of as a lunatic and troublemaker.

John the Baptist was an oddity in the desert.

Even the disciples never quite got what Jesus was up to until after His resurrection.

A few years ago we had a special concert at our church by the contemporary Christian artist, Dana Russell. She and I had just finished working together on a conference event, and I was helping her pack up Sunday afternoon to head to my church. She walked up to me and said, "Jim, I need to talk with you. God is laying something really weird on my heart."

Dana, her husband, and I went into their camper and sat down. She said, "I'll just tell you. I believe God is calling us to have a foot washing at your church tonight. He has never asked me to do that before, so I wanted to lay it on you and find out what you think."

Keep in mind. This was on the heels of a very intensive weekend during which the leadership gets about 4 hours of sleep each night. Though I had done foot washings on a number of occasions -not in *that* church as of yet- I really was not in the mood for doing anything out of the ordinary. My response was, "Dana, I'm the wrong guy to ask. I'm tired. You call God back and tell Him that He has the wrong number."

After a little laughter, and jumping back and forth through some other topics, we finally agreed to pray about it between that time and the concert and see if God would give me a clear leading.

As the concert approached that evening, I became more and more apprehensive. My main concern was how would we do a foot washing for over three hundred people. By the time Dana arrived, I had not received a great "revelation" from God. To tell you the truth, at that point, God may have been trying to give me a revelation, I just wasn't picking up the phone. After a little more discussion between Dana and myself, we decided to get everything ready for a possible foot washing and hope that the Lord would give a clear leading during the concert. The problem was that all we were able to find was *one* large washing tub. I remember asking much the same question Andrew asked of Jesus when he handed Jesus the loaves and fish, "But how far will so few go among so many?" (John 6:9)

The concert went along as expected. Through Dana's special God-given gifts the people were lifted up, brought to the throne, and introduced to the Lord. It was a wonderful and moving experience, during which, I sat in the back saying, "Lord, please don't make us do a foot washing. Lord, please don't make us do a foot washing."

Near the close of her concert, Dana started sharing her testimony and then talked about "letting the Lord cleanse you." She gave an invitation for everyone to receive whatever cleansing they needed to receive from God; whether it be a cleansing from sin, from guilt, from fear, whatever. They could leave that night washed and freed.

During the quiet time, she walked back to me and asked, "Well, what do you think?"

I said, "I have been sitting here having a good old-fashioned argument with God. I'm still not in the mood, but the only thing that keeps running through my mind is that there are people here who need to be cleansed. That's all I know. I feel very strongly that there are people here who need to be cleansed."

The words were barely out of my mouth, when a big smile came across her face, her eyes lit up and she said, "Okay! That's good enough for me!" She abruptly turned away and headed back to the stage to start the foot washing.

I personally wanted to throw up. I was still wondering how we were going to do it logistically. God's directions to her were to close the formal concert and then invite anyone who wanted to leave whatever they surrendered earlier, to remove their shoes and we -Dana and I- would wipe a damp rag across their feet as they went out the main door. We took our places on either side of our one tub and started releasing the crowd row by row.

I was amazed! I was amazed at the people who came out with tears in their eyes and their shoes in their hands. Little old ladies and the strong scraping men of my church, came out visibly touched, wanting -needing- to have their feet washed and their spirit touched by the breath of God. What really bowled me over, was that while I was sitting in the back, prior to the foot washing, I kept wishing that certain people in my congregation would have been there because of their desperate need for a real cleansing in their lives. During the concert, I looked and hoped, but I could not find them in the crowd. I did not have to see them. God saw them. Every one of those who ran across my mind were present that night; and everyone of them came out with their shoes off.

Praise the Lord!

Ah! Wait! This happy ending story is not to imply that no one came out disgusted with what was going on. For whatever reason, there was a large number of people who did not appreciate what we were doing and I was very certain that I would never see them cross the threshold of that church as long as I was still the pastor. But it did not matter. As I knelt there next to Dana, washing the feet of people with tears in their eyes, I looked over at her, she caught my eye and asked, "Are you embarrassed?"

My response surprised me. I said, "No, This is great. It feels so.... so, natural."

Oh, if only the lesson from that night would sink into my thick skull and selfish heart permanently. I'm still working on getting out of the picture. But, as I do, the more **obedience** becomes a natural result.

Jerry Sittzer said it well what those who are becoming immersed come to know as the truth. He said:

> "Obedience is the logical response to three indisputable facts: God is *sovereign*, having the ability to give us the best; God is *good*, desiring to

give us the best; God is *wise*, knowing what that best is and telling us so in the Bible. Obedience enables us to live in harmony with these facts. Disobedience challenges them and so leads to death.

Obedience is an investment in absolute reality. It is a way of affirming that God is true and trustworthy and that He has designed life to be lived a certain way.

We cannot obey God if we do not believe He is truly God. If God is God, obedience makes sense. If He is not, it is insane."

CHAPTER 13
A Calm in the Storm

"Peace I leave with you; my peace I give you. I do not give to you as the world gives. Do not let your hearts be troubled and do not be afraid." (John 14:27 NIV)

Just prior to taking my first church, which I served during seminary, there was a dynamic young girl in that church who died in a tragic car wreck. She was one of those types who had everything going for her. She was beautiful, intelligent, witty, creative, had a wonderful family, and most importantly, knew Jesus Christ. She was sixteen years old, driving down one of the back roads in her area and made the mistake of reaching over into the passenger floor board to pick up a cassette tape. When she did, the car veered to the right, went off the edge of the pavement, went out of control, and finally slammed into a tree. The community was shaken. Literally hundreds turned out for the funeral. I heard that there were people who were standing outside the windows, peering into the church because the seating was taken an hour before the service began.

Throughout the next three years I spent time with the family and did my bumbling best to help them deal with their loss. It was somewhere in my second year that the mother told me the following story:

> I had made it no secret over the years that I was a Christian. There were many times I would talk with my co-workers about church and the struggles of following Christ in the world. There was this one woman who was a constant cynic to our group. She was always throwing in ridiculous questions, or intentionally trying to irritate us to see how far she could push us before we broke. None of us were very disappointed when she quit and found a job somewhere else.

A few months ago I was in the main office when I saw her standing by the counter. I did not think she would recognize me, much less start up a conversation with me, so I was very surprised when she started walking in my direction. The first thing out of her mouth was, "You're one of those Christian, church goers aren't you?"

I said, "Yes."

She said, "Aren't you the one who lost a daughter about a year ago?"

Again, I said, "Yes."

Her next question blew my mind. She asked with a very cynical and snotty tone, "Well, where did all that Christian stuff get you, huh?"

I stood there for a few seconds contemplating ways that I could destroy her and hide the body. I could not believe that anyone -Christian or NON- could be so callous and cold. After a quick prayer, I regained my composure, a smile crept across my face and I said, "I'm standing here aren't I?"

Then it hit me! God was exactly the reason I was still standing. My life had been torn apart, and everything I believed in had been challenged. Yet, through it all, there was always the indescribable presence of..... peace.

Peace. The old 60's song says that what the world needs now is love. I would agree. But second on the list of what the world needs now is *Peace*. And I will go on record as saying that the only place we will ever find that peace will be when we are totally immersed in the Spirit of God. We can look everywhere, but peace is nowhere to be found except in the loving arms of Jesus.

This is what Paul said about the subject:

"Rejoice in the Lord always, I will say it again: Rejoice! Let your gentleness be evident to all. The Lord is near. Do not be anxious about anything, but in everything, by prayer and petition, with thanksgiving, present your requests to God. And the peace of God, which transcends all understanding, will guard your hearts and your minds in Christ Jesus." (Phillipians 4:4-7)

Peace. The world needs it, but so few of us really understand it. Go back and read the quote from Phillipians. Even Paul admits that this peace of God is beyond our understanding. If it is beyond our understanding, you can rest assured it is going to be beyond our *explanation* as well. What then *is* this peace of God that is available when we become immersed in His Spirit?

I can tell you better what it is **not**.

Everyone Being Happy

First of all, this peace is not everyone being happy, as many believe.

When we first hear the word "peace," we think of gentle breezes blowing over waving meadows in the middle of summer vacation. The kids are all playing nicely on the swings, the dog is laying lazily at our side, and our spouse is going to the cooler to get us an ice cold soda. Peace means that we are safe and out of harms way.

That situation is *peace-full*. At that moment in time, all does seem right with the world. But, let one child accidentally bump the other with a swing; let the dog catch the scent of a rabbit; let that colony of ants finally burrow through your ground cover, and your peace-filled situation turns to chaos. The peace that Paul is talking about; the peace that is mentioned in connection with those who are surrendered to Jesus, is *not* contingent on a person's *external situation*.

Rocking The Boat

This indescribable peace is also not a matter of avoiding having one's boat rocked.

Over the years I have heard a number of ministers -myself included- who had gone through some major controversy in their church say things like, "Everything is finally calming down. There is at least a little time of peace for all of us to catch our breath." *That* is not peace. That is especially not the peace Jesus left us. The type of peace this kind of remark is describing is a lack of anyone outwardly rocking the boat or bucking the system. If we use that criteria to judge whether something is peaceful, then China could be considered a country at peace. It was those Tiananmen Square radicals who stirred up the hornet's nest and caused the fuss. It took the government to come in and either imprison, torture, reprogram, or kill the dissenters for there to be "peace," a lack of boat rocking.

I don't think that is what either Jesus or Paul had in mind when they talked about peace.

Getting My Way

The peace of God is also not someone getting his or her way.

One of the big selling points for those who like to preach the very profitable "Gospel of Prosperity" is that if we give our lives to Jesus, we will get everything our little, spoiled rotten hearts desire. It does not matter what is going on in the rest of the world, or if what you want has any ill effects on anyone around you, the important question is are *you* satisfied and is everything going *your* way. "When that is the case," the lie goes, "*then* you will be at peace." This has a great deal to do with the old adage, "The squeaky wheel gets the grease." I don't know how many times I have sat in meetings where there has been some ridiculous fuss made by one person over some petty personal agenda. After a long and drawn out discussion, almost always someone will suggest: "Why don't we just let them have their way so that we can get a little peace around here?"

In other words, the ministry of the church and everyone else's needs will go unmet as long as the one with the biggest mouth and most obnoxious attitude gets her way. Is that peace? If you ask the person with the big mouth and obnoxious attitude, that person would enthusiastically say, "Yes!"

None of these are the peace Jesus was talking about.

Do you see a common thread running through each of these frequently held descriptions of peace? It is the lack of **external conflict**. In other words, our primary understanding of peace is based on whether everything around us is "correct", or "right" for us. If everything is, then we will be at peace.

WRONG!!

Though some may read this as a rationalization, the truth is that the peace of God is a peace that is completely unrelated to our external circumstances. Read again the first sentence quoted from Phillipians: "Rejoice in the Lord always." The key word is "always". Paul did not say, "Rejoice in the Lord when everything is going well and you are getting whatever you want." He said, "Rejoice in the Lord always"....despite the external circumstances you now face. It is when you can do *that*, that you truly have the peace of God.

What then is this peace of God which transcends all understanding? Simply put, it is a calmness in the midst of a storm. Think about many of the things covered in this book to this point. If they are present and active in our souls, calmness in the midst of a storm will be the natural result. If we find our value in God, then when the world is telling us we are worthless, instead of knocking ourselves out to please a society which will never be satisfied, we have a calmness which enables us to stand firm.

If we find power immersed in the Spirit of God, then when the road blocks come (and come they will) and we start to "tucker out", we can rest in the peace that if God wants it done, He will give us the ability to go on.

If we are truly able to say, "Not my will but Thine," then when the world calls us fools, dreamers, and fanatics, we can be at peace that we know where the hash marks are and where we are heading.

IF we are truly getting out of the picture and being immersed in the Spirit of God, the garbage of the world has little, if *any* influence on our lives. In the midst of the storm, we can experience calm. Why? Because, just like the disciples discovered on that stormy night on the sea of Galilee, we exist in the presence of the one who even commands the elements! (Matthew 8:23-27)

One of my favorite, "awe shucks", cute kid, examples of peace is one I heard about a young boy who had been given a special ring by his mother. A few years later his mother died and the ring became even more precious to him than before. One day, the boy lost the ring and consequently went into a panic. With tears streaming down his face, he tore the house apart looking for it. The more he looked, the more panicked he became, and the more he cried. Suddenly, he remembered what his mom used to tell him, "Son, never forget to pray and give everything over to Jesus." The boy stopped dead in his tracks, bowed his head, and gave the situation over to Jesus. At that very moment he stopped crying and became calm.

His older brother, as most older brothers do, was getting a sick pleasure out of watching his younger brother suffer. The older brother happened to see the younger one stop and pray. The older brother said cynically, "What are you doing? Do you think if you pray God will show you where the ring is?"

The younger brother looked at the other with very calm eyes and said, "I don't know. But I do know this: It has made me quite willing to be without it if that is God's will, and isn't that just as good as having it?"

Peace. Calm in the midst of the storm because we walk with the one who has made the path that is best for us.

"Yeah, though I walk through the valley of the shadow of death, I will fear no evil for *Thou art with me*." (Psalm 23:4)

In the eighteenth century there was a very prominent man who quite literally had everything. By the standards of *any* time his life was perfect. He had a wonderful family, a well-paying job, and a strong relationship with God. Then one day, much like Job, a message came that his family and all that he held precious had been destroyed in a shipwreck at sea. He truly entered into the valley of the shadow of death.

What would have been your response? Most of us would have become bitter, angry, and fallen into deep depression and despair. I don't doubt that he struggled with those feelings as well. However, *if* he *did* struggle in the valley of death and doubt, he did not stay there long. Later that same man penned these words of hope and peace: "When peace like a river attendeth my way; when sorrow like sea billows roll; whatever my lot, Thou has taught me to say, it is well, it is well with my soul." ("It Is Well With My Soul" by Horatio G. Spafford)

Peace. A calm in the mist of a storm.

When my father died, I felt a very strong need to take part in the memorial service. Too many times I had listened to ministers give a generic funeral eulogy where it was obvious that they had taken a pre-packaged sermon and simply inserted the name of the deceased in the appropriate places. Though I knew that the persons who were going to speak at my father's memorial service would not do that, I still felt a need for there to be some specific sentiments shared on behalf of the family.

There were at least 1800 people present at the service. The church had set up cameras in the main sanctuary of my dad's church and were showing the service to the overflow crowd on a big screen television in the fellowship hall. Needless to say, I was a tad nervous. Not only was it the largest crowd I had ever addressed, which included a few bishops and almost the entire Cabinet of the Florida conference, but I was about to stand up and speak at my *father's* funeral. I remember sitting with the family during the first portion of the service, becoming aware that my heart rate was slowly increasing. There was one point where I knew that if a heart attack did not kill me, I would probably die from dehydration because of how much I was sweating.

I had been praying like crazy for about 3 days. I was asking God for help. I had begged God for the right words to say, and the strength to say them. I had asked him how I could be so stupid as to volunteer to do what I was about to do. Though I knew God had given me the words, and that His Spirit was in the room, I was still a basket case. Then it hit me. From out of the blue, an almost audible voice said, "Rest. Rest."

Nothing more. There was no, "Rest, I'm here. You'll do wonderful." Just simply, "Rest." I did not see angels and the service did not draw to a sudden close. I simply heard the word "Rest" repeated over and over.

So I rested. I put my notes to the side, closed my eyes, bowed my head, and even slumped in the pew a little in order to get comfortable. If I would have had a pillow, I probably would have laid down right then and there. If I have learned anything, it is to take the Lord as literally as I can.

Almost the second I let go, I felt an overwhelming presence envelope me. If I would have been willing to open my eyes, I might have found that I was floating a few inches above the pew. It sure felt like I was. It was not a feeling of euphoria or "happiness", however. The only description I have been able to come up with after eleven years is that it felt like a soothing blanket of calm being wrapped around my body and soul. In the midst of the storm, God gave me a calm.... a peace. And these words came to mind, and finally found their meaning: "He makes me lie down in green pastures, he leads me beside the quiet waters, he restores my soul." (Psalms 23:2,3a)

Peace.

The word has the same root meaning as the Hebrew word "Shalom" -wholeness, completeness. Peace is not something we search for in order to find God. Peace is that total sense of wholeness, completeness, which finds us when we are immersed in the presence of God.

CHAPTER 14

A Reason To Smile

"Though you have not seen him, you love him; and even though you do not see him now, you believe in him and are filled with an inexpressible and glorious joy,...." (I Peter 1:8)

When I was in high school, the group I hung out with was just like any other typical bunch of high school teens. We had basically the same worries, same joys, same goals.... same hormones as everyone else. I remember thinking the world was coming to an end whenever I found a pimple on my face, which was often. I remember sitting in the floor of my kitchen and dialing one particular girl's number at least 100 times trying to get up enough nerve to ask her out on a date. I remember my first love, my first kiss, and all of the great times that tend to sweep us back into the wonderful world of nostalgia when we talk about "the good ole' days".

The reason I bring up this trip down memory lane is to say that I really did not know anything was missing. Like I said, the crowd I hung out with looked and acted a lot like everyone else looked and acted. We were not quite as cool as the Fonz or as hip as the Bee Gees, but we had our moments every now and then. However, I clearly recall the summer prior to my sophomore year in high school when my eyes were finally opened to the fact that *something* was missing.

The eye opening situation came when I attended a Christian camp with my father who was scheduled to be the speaker for the week. As we were making our way to camp, I had visions of nerdy Christians running around with their Bibles under their arms, trying to see who could out quote the other in scripture. Obviously, I was not a Christian at the time.

Once I arrived at the camp, although I tried to avoid contact with "those people" (Christians), I almost immediately ran into four kids who struck me as a little different. Actually, "different" was not the word I used at the time to describe them. They were down right weird! What made them so weird -in my humble opinion- was that they seemed to have a certain...... "lightness" about them. Others might have described it as "joy", but "lightness" says it best for me.

Up until that point, most of the people I had hung around smiled, laughed, and had their fair share of good times. But there always seemed to be a seriousness,.... a heaviness about them. The same was true for many of the adults I was exposed to. Gainesville, Florida was such a busy place, that everyone seemed a tad rushed and overwhelmed. It could have simply been that they were rushing to get away from me, but that would be an entirely different story.

Anyway, back to the "lightness" of these four teens. I noticed from the start, that it did not matter what the situation was, they seemed to approach it with a sense of anticipation and joy. Two of the four did not have much materially speaking, but that did not seem to embarrass them or bring them down in the least. The other two were preacher's kids (not being very wealthy and being a preacher's kid is bad enough to ruin anyone's personality), but none of that seemed to matter. They were filled with..... -if I may quote- "an inexpressible and glorious joy." Simply put, they laughed at everything!

The first time I laid eyes on this bunch, they were in a cafe, literally rolling on the floor under a table with laughter. I do not know what the joke was, but nothing could have been *that* funny. Later, after I had reluctantly started hanging out with them -purely out of curiosity mind you- one of the guys came falling down the steps, plopped on the floor in what I know was a painful heap, stood up, brushed himself off and said, "Well, like the Predestinarian said, 'I'm glad that's over.'" We laughed.

There were a number of the other youth on the grounds who did not appreciate the personality of these four kids.....

plus one. When one or two of these other kids would go out of their way to call us names, or pull a prank on us, my first reaction was to push those kids out into traffic and tell God they slipped. The other four's reaction was uniformly, "Ah, what difference does it make. There's no way we could make him more miserable than he already is."

They were filled with an inexpressible and glorious joy! In fact, it was that evident joy that ultimately drew me to the Lord. It is that evident joy that is present, prevalent, and waiting for those who are getting out of the picture and are being immersed in the Spirit of God.

I am not sure who started it, but the person or persons who pushed the ridiculous idea that Christians are to be somber, sad looking, sour pusses, really ought to be taken out behind the barn and tickled to death. If there is anything in this world that truly brings *real* and *lasting* joy, it is knowing Jesus Christ. Wasn't it Jesus who said, "I have come that they may have life and have it more abundantly"? (John 10:10) YES it was! And abundant life is not communicated by an expression you might find on someone who looks as if they have been buying their underwear a size too small. Abundant life is communicated by a life and countenance filled with joy and celebration.

Let me qualify something before I go on. I am not *at all* talking about those silly, misguided people who think real Christians must walk around with ridiculous grins on their faces saying things like, "I know I just lost my leg, my child is dying, and my dog has fleas..... But praise the Lord, I'm a happy camper!" I not only do not trust that type of "faith", but I have often seen that type of total disregard for reality come crashing down around many of those "I'm so happy" Christians.

Nor am I talking about the immature person who makes a joke out of everything and is completely insensitive to the suffering and pain of others. One of the most nauseating things I have to go through as a pastor is sharing the responsibility of doing a funeral with another minister who likes to sit around before the service telling jokes and laughing. Even if I was not personally touched by the loss of the person I was doing a service for, common courtesy would dictate that I would not be in the wings laughing while the family is waiting outside.

What I am talking about; what Paul was trying to emphasize, and what I am daily coming to know as I continue to move out of the picture is what it means to enJOY life!

I have made a number of conditional statements before in this book, and I will make another now: **We can not know joy, and we can not enjoy life, until we know Jesus Christ and take part in the process of being immersed in His spirit.**

Admittedly, though, "joy" is a rather vague word in our day and time. What *would* an immersed life filled with joy look like?

As I was thinking and praying about that question, I became rather stumped myself in my attempt to find a one line definition of joy. The more I thought about it, the more I realized joy is actually a combination of attributes thrown together in one glorious mess.

"Then what are the attributes?" you ask.

Good question. Here they are:

Peace

The joy which comes by being immersed in the Spirit of God consists of the peace described in the previous chapter. Since you just finished reading a chapter on peace, I will not beat the issue to death. If you need to, go back and read it again.

Contentment

Godly, holy joy consists of contentment.

There's a lady I have known for years who has a real problem experiencing this wonderful joy of immersion primarily because of the lack of *this* element: contentment. Simply put, she just cannot be satisfied with the way things are or what she has. She grew up as a mill worker's daughter and, by her own admission, never had very much. All of her early life she dreamed of marrying someone who would be able to afford all of the fancy luxuries of life. Yet, she made the fatal mistake of marrying for love and wound up with an inner city social worker. If you have lived on this planet for very long, you will know that inner city social workers do not make a truck load of money. In fact, I'm sad to say, they barely make a wheelbarrow load of money. Needless to say, she does not have all of the fancy luxuries of life. That has not stopped her from wanting them though. If she has a decent car, she will want one a little nicer and a bit bigger. If she has a car a little nicer and a bit bigger, after awhile she'll want a mini-van. If she is working in production at the factory, she wants to work in advertising. If she's working in advertising, she doesn't want to work with the people she's working with. If she *does* get with the people she wants to work with, after awhile she'll want to be in product development.

You get the point. In many ways, she is growing deeper in her relationship with God. She *is* slowly getting out of the picture in many aspects of her life and consequently is the poster child for much of what is contained in this chapter. But, her lack of contentment is what is holding her back from experiencing completely this "inexplicable and glorious joy." She just does not know how to be satisfied.... yet.

Don't get me wrong. I'm not saying that contentment is just lying down where you are and never wanting to make a change. That could be laziness or apathy. One of the things which has frustrated me the most in my ministry over the years has been the people who are content to have shallow religiosity and see absolutely no need to change. That is not the contentment I am talking about. Never wanting to grow or better one's self is cowardly and pathetic. It is my lack of contentment concerning the depth of my faith that constantly pushes me forward toward God.

By "contentment" I mean the ability to take a situation as is and do your best with it, knowing that God is ultimately in charge. I guess the "serenity prayer" communicates best what I mean by contentment:

> "Lord, grant me the serenity to accept the things I cannot change,
> The courage to change the things I can,
> And the wisdom to know the difference."

For years, while I served on a multi-church charge, I had a hard time truly knowing this joy primarily because of my lack of contentment. The serenity prayer made absolutely no sense to me. I figured that if I worked hard enough, visited frequently enough, and prepared earth shattering sermons, the community would beat a path to the church's door and there would be great growth.... all to the glory of the Kingdom, of course. It didn't work. The more I tried, the more I floundered. Then I began to discover what is in this book; what it means to get out of the picture and be fully immersed in God.

One of the first things God said to me when I began to be able to hear Him better was that I was where *He* wanted me to be. He said, "Work hard. Do your best. Look to the future and have great visions of people knowing me, but *your* job is to till the soil and scatter the seed where you are. *"My job,"* God said, "is to bring forth the fruit." In hearing that, contentment swept over me like waves on the shore. My job was not to improve my situation by what I could do. My job was to do what I could, empowered by The Spirit, and leave the rest to Him.

I finally figured out what C.T. Studd meant when he wrote, "Some people want to live within the sound of church or chapel bells. I want to run a rescue shop within three feet of hell."

117

WOW! He could only say that if he was content not to be famous, but to be in the presence of God and where God wanted him to be.

There is great joy there!

Excitement

The joy found in being immersed in the Spirit of God carries with it a sense of excitement and anticipation.

One of the sad attributes that many people have is that we are a jaded, callous people. In today's terms, "It's just not cool to get excited about anything." That was one of the things I very clearly remember about my high school experience. If the youth director or group leader would say, "All right everyone, we're going to take a shuttle to Mars!", the appropriately cool response would be, "Whoopee. How boring. Sorry, I have to wash my hair."

It did not matter whether you were personally excited about it or not. The "in dude" response to everything was to imply that you had already done it all and were bored with life. The modern parallel is the remark "Been there. Done that. Bought a T-shirt." Yet, one of the things which first turned me off -because it was not cool- but later really turned me on about the four kids at the camp was that they were excited about everything! Someone would suggest we take a walk around the lake, and everyone would say, "Yeah! That sounds great!" Someone else would recommend a game of four square, and there would immediately be a mad rush out the door toward the court. They seemed ready and enthusiastic about everything.

Know what? It was contagious. What I mean is, not only did I get excited when they got excited, but everything we did with that enthusiastic spirit, we enjoyed.

Godly joy has excitement about what *could be* and *will be* because God is in charge.

Childlike Wonder

Holy joy has within it a sense of childlike wonder.

The absence of this wonder gets back again to our jaded and callused society. There are few things more discouraging to me than taking a group of youth out on the Appalachian Trail, and while looking at a breath taking view hear them say, "You know, it's too bad all of this can't be screened in so that we can enjoy it more. Where's the bathroom anyway?"

Likewise, there are few things which touch my soul and bring a smile to my face more than walking with my child on a wooded path only to find myself walking alone. I turn around and see that she has stopped to watch a ladybug crawl across a blade of grass or to watch a spider spin a web. I make my way back to her and she says, "Look Daddy! Look at the colors! Look at what it's doing!" In that moment, I can easily sense that she appreciates and values ALL of the world around her; even the little, supposedly insignificant things.

When we are getting out of the picture and are immersed in the Spirit of God, we become keenly aware of the wonders of His creation and instinctively marvel at them. There is no true joy that does not have a sense of childlike wonder attached to it.

Lightness

I have to use the word "lightness" again. Though it is not the most theologically sounding word, nor is it grammatically correct, it communicates a great deal.

What I mean by "lightness" is not taking the world or yourself too seriously. We like to attribute the trait of emotional overreaction only to teenagers. SORRY! Teenagers are simply *advertised* as more emotional about everything. I have found that *adults* tend to overreact much more and to a deeper, more dangerous degree than any teen.

For example, I used to help run a camp in the rural mountains of North Carolina. My job was to put the camp in tip-top condition and help with the rental process. The rental agreement was that each group would pay a $25 deposit up front and then the remainder of the fee on arrival. After a group left, my job was to go in behind them and make sure everything was clean and in working order. If anything had to be done, the cost would be taken out of the $25 deposit.

One weekend we had a local group rent the camp as they had done many times in the past. About the time they were leaving, another group was coming in to use the camp on a day use basis. I arrived to check the camp about 20 minutes after the "day use" group had arrived. By the time I arrived, the day use group was already in the pool and using the basketball court. I waved as I passed by and made my way into the main lodge to begin my regular check. The main room was in pretty good condition. I had seen better, and I had definitely seen worse. For the most part, it was acceptable. The grounds had a bit of trash here and there, but the real problem was in the bathrooms. They were pretty messed up. I made note of the conditions, went home and contacted the people who usually came to clean. I deducted the $10 it would cost to clean everything, and sent the remaining $15 back to the weekend renting group with a note explaining the missing $10.

About three days later I received a call from the pastor asking if I could come and meet with a few of the leaders in his church the next day. He seemed rather pleasant on the phone, so I assumed it had to do with future use of the facilities. Buddy! I was WRONG!! In the words of that pastor and the three other leaders from his church who were present at our meeting, they were "devastated by what I had done."

To be honest, I did not know what they were talking about at first. What in the world had I done that would have "devastated" them.

By the way, when they said "devastated" they said it with one of those big sighs; like "De (let out lots of air) vessta (let out more air) ted."

I turned a little red with embarrassment, and asked them what had happened. They then proceeded to inform me how insulted they were that I would ever imply that *they* had not adequately cleaned up after themselves. Each of the leaders then gave me a lengthy step-by-step break down of how they covered every inch of that place and "How dare you accuse us of not cleaning the facilities! We have a good mind to report you and never use that camp again."

I sat there with my jaw on the floor wondering if Alan Funt from Candid Camera was going to step out from behind the door. I could not believe these people were serious. It was at this point that one from this lovingly mature group mentioned that there had been another group which had come in as their group was leaving and that *they* -emphasis on "they"-could have very well used the bathrooms for changing.

That thought had briefly crossed my mind while they were berating me, but I had dismissed it due to the fact that there was ample changing room at the bath houses and much of the mess in the bathrooms was dry. I know things dry quickly in the summer heat, but give me a break. Not wanting to get into a major confrontation over $10, however, I conceded that the other group *could have* made the mess, and that I was sorry that I had implied any terribly defaming disrespect to their church and its good reputation.

I actually did not say it that way, but I really wish I had.

I told them I would immediately return the $10, and stood up to leave, thinking that was the end of it. Then the most ridiculous thing I had ever heard was said to me. Truthfully, the remark was not as absurd as the reason the minister said it. He said, "Please sit down." I sat. He continued, "I just want to say that if you are so insensitive and unfeeling towards other's feeling, you have no business being in the ministry. I think you ought to find another job."

Again, I thought he was going to smile. "He couldn't be serious!" I thought to myself. But, alas, he was. I figured I better get myself out of that office before they cut up a chicken and poured its innards on my head, or something to that effect.

At first I was pretty upset when I finally escaped the group's clutches, . Then I realized that these were some very sad people and that I should really be in prayer *for* them instead of getting upset *by* them. I can say this though, it was for people like that the phrase "Lighten up!" was coined.

Godly joy knows of a God who is in charge and, consequently, is enabled to see that things are not as bad or big as we tend to make them.

Playfulness

Lastly, "out of the picture" joy has an ever growing quality of playfulness in it. By playfulness, I mean the tendency to draw others into your joy and just have fun.

I know this is not the deepest insight you may have ever read, but it is the truth nonetheless. If there is anyone in the world who should have fun in this life, it should be a Christian. If Christians are not having fun, it is either because they are not really Christians but just religious and do not know Jesus Christ, OR their shoes are too tight. Souls resting in the Spirit of the Lord of laughter know what it means to play.

The best example of this for me was my father. By all standards, my father was a nut. If he did not have the excuse of belonging to Christ as a way to explain his strange behavior, he probably would have been put in a mental hospital. He loved to play, and he loved to draw others into his playfulness. I am glad to say that I have been accused of having some of the same qualities.

When I went to my second church appointment out of seminary, there were a number of people who were a little "disturbed" at my playfulness. A few of them decided that it was immaturity -which probably *did* have something to do with it- and that I would eventually grow out of it. I informed them during an official Administrative Board meeting that, especially in the Martin family, the "immaturity" only gets worse, not better. At the end of my four years at that charge, one of the ladies who had been the most concerned about my "immaturity" came up to me on my last Sunday, took me by the shoulders, looked right into my eyes and simply said, "You're right. It gets worse."

Since then I have decided that "Christian playfulness" will always be considered immaturity if you are under 30 years old. Once you hit your mid-30's through the early 60's it will be considered "charm". After 65 or so, this playfulness will be considered senility. You have now been officially forewarned.

And you will be ".....filled with an inexpressible and glorious joy."

Amen! Let it shine!

Jesus called us the "light of the world". I do not know of many things which shine brighter than a joy-filled life.

Remember though, it is only when we are being fully immersed in the Spirit of God that we find that joy.

Getting over the wall

*"Many....said, 'This is a hard teaching. Who can accept it"
(John 6:60 NIV)*

Interesting scripture to start off a new section, don't you think?

The background to John 6:60 is very simple. Jesus was doing all the things which made Jesus a "huthold name" around Israel. Everywhere you turned, Jesus was healing the sick, exorcising the demons, and generally being an everyday miracle working Messiah. The people loved him! The people especially loved the way he would put the religious leaders in their place. No one like Jesus had the knack for turning the Pharisees' trick questions back on themselves. It seemed every time Jesus finished speaking, the Scribes and Pharisees walked away with their jaws hanging open and the people left snickering with delight.

All was right with the world, until Jesus started getting a little radical, according to the taste of the general populace. As long as Jesus performed great works for the people, kept the intellectuals at bay, and stayed in the shallows of religiosity, everything was hunky-dory. But Jesus, being Jesus, couldn't leave well enough alone. He started shaking the trees of the fundamentalists too much. John captures one of the best examples of this over-exuberant tree shaking in his Gospel account.

Just prior to John 6:60, Jesus refers to himself as the bread of life. Jesus didn't let it rest with just *that* statement, however. He went on to boldly proclaim himself as the *only way* to a relationship with the Father. As far as the general populace was concerned, it was all downhill from there. Possibly, the straw which broke the camel's back was when Jesus started getting a little too graphic with his analogies and talked about the people eating his flesh and drinking his blood. Not only was this imagery a tad disgusting, but it appeared Jesus was telling the people that they had to be immersed in *His* presence and filled with *His* Spirit if they were ever going to know eternal life and have a relationship with God.

Too much was too much. That "only way" and "full surrender" stuff went way beyond a few moral laws and some guidelines about keeping your teeth clean and your breath fresh. The people wanted no part of such radical teaching. So, they did what any non-thinking, shallowly religious, "go along with the majority" crowd would do; they turned tail and walked away. They deserted Jesus.

Times have not changed much. The preferred choice of the majority of people is still to stay in the shallows. It has always been, and will always be, more popular to stay where it's safe; where little is asked of us and even less is expected, than to press out where things might get a little hairy and we might possibly get hurt.

Do you want to lose friends and turn people off? Talk to them about commitment and devotion. Do you want to *really* irritate modern day Americans? Point down a narrow path and say something radical like, "That is the *only* road you can take to get where you truly want and need to go. You don't have a choice, and the path is not as easy as it looks."

Not a popular disclosure....then or now. We want to walk the path of least resistance.

I was talking with a friend the other day about this very topic. With a laugh, we both agreed that we are so desperate to feel comfortable and secure here and now that we will support any organization which makes us feel good now even if we are being sold a shallow lie. But let anyone point to a leak in the walls of the dam holding back the floodwaters, and we stick our fingers in our ears and call them pessimists and doom-sayers.

A good example of this was the raging debate concerning the national debt. During the 80's we were skillfully told that we could have our cake and eat it too. Our country kept borrowing and borrowing from the global banks in order to pay for the band so we could keep on dancing at the party. The few groups who kept raising their hands and asking where the money was coming from were shot down as negative and anti-American. As a country, we kept the party going by not caring who was stuck with the bill as long as we were comfortable now.

People still have not opened their eyes to the dangers this country faces due to our overspending and consequent huge national debt. We still want to live in a state of ignorance as long as we can feel good about *now*. But somewhere, somehow, someone is going to have to pay back the trillions of dollars this country owes to the band who played so that we could dance for so long. The standard response to this type of statement? "Don't rain on my parade. My business is doing fine....now."

Will we ever learn?

We want financial comfort...., moral comfort......, social comfort....why not religious comfort. We want the path of least resistance. We want what will have the fewest expectations. Anyone who points to a leaking dike, or anything which calls us beyond our comfort zone, we label as radical, restrictive, and either ignore it, or try to kill it.

A gentleman in one of my earlier appointments expressed the majority sentiment best. He said, "Preacher, don't get too fanatical. Just preach a good sermon, visit the sick, and don't rock the boat. Things are going pretty good around here. No need to fix what ain't broke."

Though I can understand the desire to take the path of least resistance and stay in the shallows where it's safe, I can't get a grasp on how people can remain comfortable following that path or building sand castles on that shore when all the time Jesus is calling us to move forward, and press out into the deep. How *can* so many ignore Jesus' call? How *do* we stay comfortable? If, throughout the Bible, God is constantly urging us to go beyond the shallows, out into deeper waters, what is it that keeps us satisfied to dance around in the foam? What *do* we use to plug our ears to His voice?

I believe I have some answers. Care to know what they are? Read on. This section is here to help name some of the "ear plugs" and to remove some of the bricks from the wall which stands between us and a fully immersed, living relationship with God; God's destination for our lives.

CHAPTER 15

The Lure Of Safe Religion

"For the time will come when men will not put up with sound doctrine. Instead, to suit their own desires, they will gather around them a great number of teachers to say what their itching ears want to hear." (II Timothy 4:3 NIV)

If there has ever been a place we can hide from the true call of God in our lives, it is in the comfortable, popular, and well regarded arms of **religion**. One of the sad aspects of being a minister today, and one of the hardest things I find to help people unlearn, is that Christianity and religion are *not* synonymous. Being religious does not make a person any more a Christian than typing into a computer makes one an accomplished writer. (Trust me! I am speaking from experience with that analogy.) Christianity is a relationship with the living God. Religion is a set of rituals one can perform in the worship of....... *anything*!! Though Christians may tend to be religious in their worship of God, being religious does not automatically imply that one worships God.

For example, sports fans are some of the most religious people I know. I would go as far as to say that most sports fans are more religious than many Christians. I know a few Redskins fans who are more devoted to, and better witnesses for their team than most people who claim to know the Son of God. Does a sports fan's religiosity make him a worshiper of God? I think not.

How about Satanists? Satanists are very religious people. A few years ago, there was an article in our area paper which described a gruesome mutilation of a calf. The police theorized that the calf had been killed for some bizarre Satanic ritual. Talk about dedicated and religious. The paper quoted a local cult expert who described the possible religious ritual for which the Satanists needed the calf's parts. I will spare you the details. Suffice it to say, I'm glad I'm not a Satanist. They are some very religious folks though. Does their religiousness make them worshipers of God or persons filled with God's Spirit? Hardly. They worship the Enemy.

Being religious *can mean* a person is very committed to something or someone. But ritual religiousness can also be a wonderful place to hide from a real, life changing call and commitment.

Jump back a few thousand years and take a look at Jesus dealing with the same problem of people hiding from real commitment in their religiosity. When Jesus dealt with the most religious people of his day he said:

> "Woe to you, teachers of the law and Pharisees, you hypocrites! You give a tenth of your spices --mint, dill and cumin. But you have neglected the more important matters of the law--justice, mercy and faithfulness. You should have practiced the latter, without neglecting the former. You blind guides! You strain out a gnat but swallow a camel."
>
> "Woe to you, teacher of the law and Pharisees, you hypocrites! You clean the outside of the cup and dish, but inside they are full of greed and self-indulgence. Blind Pharisee! First clean the inside of the cup and dish, and then the outside also will be clean."
>
> "Woe to you, teacher of the law and Pharisees, you hypocrites! You are like whitewashed tombs, which look beautiful on the outside but on the inside are full of dead men's bones and everything unclean. In the same way, on the outside you appear to people as righteous but on the inside you are full of hypocrisy and wickedness." (Matthew 23:23-28 NIV)

What was his point? Simple: The Pharisees' interest was keeping the letter of the law. If the law said not to work on the Sabbath, then they felt it their duty to spend much of their time defining work. It mattered very little to them whether the poor or widowed were starving to death, *or* whether they were missing the Messiah, standing right under their collective noses. Keeping the letter of the law was all that mattered. Because of their shallow religiosity, they entirely missed God's greatest blessing!

The sad thing to admit is that the tendency to hide in religiousness is very common. Here is a hypothetical "for instance" that is probably closer to the truth than most of us would care to admit.

For this purely hypothetical illustration, we will use First Pentecostal church of the Squirrel Tail in Podunk, Arkansas. Podunk is located in a sleepy little farming town in rural Arkansas. The primary need of the community is food. They need it physically and spiritually. The rains have been bad, the market is slumping, and the big businesses are not moving in. People are concerned about their families' survival.

First Pentecostal Church of the Squirrel Tail has always been *the* church in the community. Farmer Jones and his family have always been "The family" of that particular church, and the church has always prided itself on being a prestigious appointment in their local conference.

Aunt Martha dies and leaves the church $3,500 in her will. That just happens to be the exact amount to replace the old, faded, moldy, rumpling carpet in the sanctuary. Or the money could be used to feed over half the constituents of the little town. The money could even go beyond a temporary solution and be used to start a lasting ministry which could provide help for the *entire* county.

A meeting of the church leaders is called. It is their responsibility to make the decisions about the church finances.

In order to squelch the tension you might be feeling as you read this, I will let you know right now, the mission outreach program did not have a snowball's chance in a very hot place. It was shot down when Susie Que Jones-Baker (Farmer Jones' daughter who married Jessie Baker) said, "Well, they bring it on themselves you know. If they worked harder.... like we do, and weren't so lazy, they wouldn't have the problem. I think we just encourage their dependency when we give them money." She followed those touching words of grace and love with, "I think if God is truly going to be glorified, we need to use my aunt's money to exalt Him by sprucing up the sanctuary."

The sanctuary sprucing idea went over unanimously.

Here is a note to the reader. If you ever want something to go over big in your church, make sure it effects the church building. Also, make sure you say things like, "With this we will exalt the Lord." There is some truth to church improvements helping in the exaltation of the Lord. Right now I can't think of anything which exalts the Lord more than gold plated toilet seats, but that is off the subject.

Everyone unanimously supported Susie Que's recommendation. The choice was between a new sound system for the pulpit or replacing the warn carpet. Since no one really wanted to be able to hear the preacher in the first place, the carpet got the nod. Now the big question. What color? Being a Florida Gator fan I have always tried to talk my churches into the orange and blue color scheme. So far I have not been successful. But I do not want to make light of this important decision. The color of a church's carpet says quite a bit about that church.

Red represents the blood of Christ. Purple stands for royalty and majesty. Maroon is..... a nice church color I guess. Blue is half way to where I think you ought to be. Green and gold mean you still live in the late 60's when every church heard the mandate from heaven to decorate their church and parsonages with a green and gold color scheme.

Susie Que suggested maroon and gray. Her husband was a graduate of the university of Georgia. There is silence. People are a little shocked. No one likes the choice. Whoever heard of using maroon and gray?

"What do we say without offending her?" they think to themselves.

"Will she get mad?" As if they did not know the answer to *that* question.

Finally a "newcomer" who somehow managed to get on the governing board says, "Well, I'm new here, but I think a nice yellow would be beautiful."

Everyone agrees enthusiastically! The vote is taken. The result is 10 for yellow and 3 against. Guess how many Joneses attended the meeting? THREE! Guess what they did? In essence, because the church did not want to play by their rules, they took their bats and balls and went home to pout!

This of course is not the end of the issue. It finally developed into the dreaded "carpet fiasco" and divided the church.

I know some of you are still having trouble with the choice of yellow. Keep in mind, this *is* a hypothetical situation.... sort of.

Let's throw a little more fuel on the fire.

In comes a new pastor. He has barely been there a day when he receives a call from a "concerned member of his flock" who wants to "share with him" some of the situations in the church he needs to "be aware of." This person comes over "for a visit" and proceeds to smear the reputation of everyone who has ever done anything of questionable result in the church. This large mouthed person -any age or sex- finally says, "And, if you hear anything about the carpet, I had nothing to do with it. I can't believe the way good Christians go behind each other's back over such issues. Now mind you, this isn't gossip. Everything I'm telling you is the truth."

After this person leaves, the minister stands there with his mouth open wondering two things: 1) What have I gotten myself into, and 2) Why *did* they choose yellow.

Actually, if the minister would have been smart, when Mr./Ms. "Holier Than Thou" started his/her trite little ravings, he should have said, "Before you get started, I've always found it best to get to know everyone on my own. By the way, have you met......" and then name some other church's minister in town in hopes he/she would start attending elsewhere.

I am obviously only scratching the surface of the examples of "gnat straining" in the local church. I do not have time to deal with dancing in the church; "Them loud youngin's who mess up everything"; or how adoption is the more preferred route for ministers to have children.

I will leave you to figure the adoption issue out for yourself. Suffice it to say that the person who shared that one with my parents said, "It (adoption) is much more pure and holy than the natural way." And I'm not making that up. Someone really said that.

The question concerning this illustration of gnat straining is: Was God exalted? Did you catch any mention of people growing deeper in their relationship with God? Do you think all the hullabaloo over carpet has ever been, or will ever be, the catalyst to launch people off the shore and into the wonderful depths of faith? "NO!" to all. But it sure makes you look terribly active.

Religiousness, gnat straining, and busy churchianity make us miss God's call to be out of the picture because we never hear that call in the first place. We become so busy with majoring on the minors and focusing on what is, by eternal standards, completely inconsequential that we miss completely what truly matters. "You strain out a gnat and swallow a camel." (Matthew 23:24 NIV)

Is this brick a part of *your* wall?

CHAPTER 16

Declarations of Faith or Mantras

"I desire mercy not sacrifice and acknowledgment of God instead of burnt offerings" (Hosea 6:6 NIV)

Now that I have established the fact that we do indeed like to stay in the shallows of safe religion, I want to take a look at some of the things which help anchor us there. Keep in mind that most of the things I will refer to are in themselves helpful and a vital part of moving deeper in one's faith and relationship with God. The problem comes when these *means* to a closer relationship with God become the *end*. These means usually become the end because they have less commitment and fewer expectations than the real thing.

CREEDS AND/OR MEMORIZED DOCTRINES

When I was in college, I worked as a youth director one summer for a Methodist church in Mobile, Alabama. We had about 60 youth in the program who came from every conceivable background imaginable. Of all the youth in the group, there was a young man named Steve who stands out in my mind to this day.

It was a Wednesday night at a Summer camp our group was attending and the speaker for the week had just finished his message and had given the altar call. The invitation was for anyone who had never given their lives to Christ to come forward and receive Him as their Lord and Savior. There were a number of teens who flocked to the front. My job was to be a "counselor," standing by in case someone at the altar wanted to talk about an issue or have someone pray with them. After everyone who wanted prayer had been prayed for, the speaker dismissed the meeting and we left for another event.

Along the path heading back to the boys' cabin I ran into Steve. What immediately had my attention about Steve was that he was doing his best to keep from looking me in the eyes. Knowing this kid, I figured the worst. Maybe he had rolled the bathrooms or hot-wired the camp tractor while everyone was at the meeting. I finally caught him, touched his shoulder, and spun him around. To my amazement he was crying. I tried to regain my composure -all the time whipping myself for thinking the worst- and I asked him what was wrong. He jerked away, gave a big sniff and said, "Nothing! Leave me alone!"

"What's wrong?" I said as I continued after him.

What he finally said has haunted me to this day. He turned, looked right at me and said, "I'll tell you what's wrong! I've been raised in the church. I know the creeds. I know the books of the Bible. I can quote a bunch of scripture. I was told that's all I need. The scripture says, 'Just believe that Jesus is who He says He is and you'll be saved.'" That was his paraphrase of Romans 10:9.

"What's wrong with me? I believe all of these things, but I know after what I heard tonight that I'm not saved!"

Go back and read that last sentence. He said, "I believe all of these things, but..." The problem is that he had been told his entire life, by well meaning teachers and preachers, that all he had to do was accept certain truths, be able to say them back as proof he had put them to memory, and then "poof," he was saved. The truth is, however, to quote another author, "You *believe* that there is one God. Good! Even the demons believe that -and shudder." (James 2:19 NIV) The point of James' remarks is that just believing something is true does not mean one has committed one's life to that truth. The saving faith Jesus talks about which leads to life, is not just believing a set of doctrines. Saving faith is, with humble trust, putting one's life into another's hands, JESUS'!

Maybe a brick in your wall is wanting "belief" to be enough because it doesn't take any amount of surrender or commitment. That may be so, but by itself it also does not lead to real life.

CEREMONY/RITUAL

The ceremonies of the church, especially The Lord's Supper and baptism, often carry dramatic power and significance in the life of the individual Christian and the church. I agree with John Wesley who believed the sacraments of communion and baptism were indeed a means of grace. He meant that through these ceremonies the Holy Spirit can and often does work wonders and touch the hearts of participants. These rituals *can be* doors through which we can be ushered into the marvelous presence of God. But, they are *not* the presence.

Read that last sentence again: "They are not the presence." While I fully see the power, potential, and significance of the ceremonies of the church, they can become the end which people seek instead of a means to The End -a deeper relationship with Christ.

A few years ago an acolyte program was established in one of the three churches I served. Because I was not at this particular church every Sunday, and the other churches did not have an acolyte program, I regularly forgot to give time for the acolyte to light the candles before the service started. As only "loving Christian folk" can do, I was gently (cough, cough) reprimanded for blatantly not allowing the acolyte time to light the candles. The first thing out of my mouth was an apology. But, before I really had time to think, the next thing out of my mouth was, "Well, you know, it's not like if we don't light the candles, we're all going to be cast into eternal damnation."

I can safely say that the person I was talking to did not think that was very funny.

Far too often we put ceremony and ritual before a living relationship if for no other reason than the fact that it's easier to participate in a ritual than it is to surrender one's life.

As I said, the rituals and ceremonies are powerful doors into the presence of God. But, they are not the Presence!

"What about baptism?" you might ask. "Aren't we saved if we're baptized?" Hardly! Not according to my experience and definitely not according to what Jesus said. He did not say, "Baptism is the way the truth and the life. No one comes to the Father but through Baptism." He said, "*I* am the way the truth and the life. No one comes to the Father but by *Me*." (John 14:15   NIV) We desperately need to get away from the lie that a person is brought into a living relationship with God through anything that person might do or have done to them by another person. Wrongfully believing that salvation comes through baptism is no different than believing it comes through good works. Either Jesus' blood was the only thing sufficient for our sins or it was not. We cannot have it both ways.

Our churches are filled with shallow religious, pitiful, baptized people who have been duped into believing a ritual will make their relationship rigtht with God. They have no concept of repentance or the need for God in their lives, much less full surrender. These people only know little beyond the fact that they went through some ritual the religious leaders said they needed to experience. These "Baptians" (instead of Christians) need to be told that they are truly missing out on what could be.

I wish I had a dime for every person who has approached me after hearing me speak over a period of time, and told me about their upbringing and their buying into the lie I just described. Some of them are mad. Some are confused. Most are relieved to know there was a reason why their "Christianity" was so meaningless and empty. The reason it was empty was that they did not know Christ. They knew only one of his ceremonies.

Baptism is a sign and symbol of an inner commitment. It is not the means to that inner commitment.

THE BIBLE

You might be a little shocked to see the Bible as a part of the section dealing with what keeps this wonderful truth of full surrender from becoming a reality in our lives. As I stated earlier, each one of these listed is intended and *can* serve as a wonderful means to the proper end. The danger is making *them* the end in themselves.

A good example of the Bible becoming the end is the person who came up to me years ago after a revival. I personally like to use a lot of scripture when I preach. I do it for two reasons: 1) I have discovered people do not hear The Word read frequently enough and so are not accustomed to turning to it instinctively as a source of help and inspiration. My perspective is if they hear a few of the wonderful gems in the Bible, it will open their eyes to the Bible's tremendous treasures. 2) If I read a lot of scripture, I do not have to prepare a very long sermon. (Hopefully you know the second reason is a joke.)

I do use a lot of scripture and encourage my listeners to follow along.

Anyway, following a revival, a gentleman approached me and said, "Son, I like the way you preach. I especially like the way you use the Bible. We need to preach the Bible more."

Before I tell you my response, can you see a problem with what that man said? Quoting his last line, "We need to preach the Bible more."

My response was, "No, we don't. We need to preach Jesus Christ. We need to use the Bible more to preach Him!"

"That's what I meant.", he said.

I said, "Yes, I thought so." I actually thought, "No, you didn't."

Regardless of what he said, he did not mean we need to preach Jesus more by using the Bible. He meant that the measure of a good sermon was how much Bible was used. That is making the means the end.

I remember attending a graveside funeral a number of years ago. Because it was a relative of someone in my church who did not attend our church, I was not asked to take part in the service. I attended out of respect for the family. There was only one minister in charge of the graveside service. I had a busy day ahead and found myself thinking, "Great! This won't take long with only one minister." Oh, was I ever wrong!! He must have read every scripture that had *any* relevance at all to death, dying, hope, suffering and how to clean out a gerbil cage. It lasted 40 minutes! My personal opinion of the service was that it was rude, insensitive, and an attempt by the minister to make himself look terribly religious and wonderfully holy by using a great deal of scripture. As I was making my way over to punch him in the nose, I overheard one of the persons in attendance say to the preacher, "That sure was a wonderful service preacher."

The person standing next to this gracious and complementary church member said, -a little too loudly- "And thank God it's over."

The Bible is a sign post to God, not a god.

I like to think of the Bible as a love letter from God to tell us about Himself. Would it be the same to marry the love letter or the lover? For example: say Elroy and Emma are engaged. Elroy is over seas for six months and writes daily of his undying love and devotion to Emma. She cherishes his letters and reads them over and over. After six months, Emma knows every dot, comma, accent, and "I love you" in all 180 letters. The big wedding day arrives, and they are standing before the minister. The minister asks Elroy all the proper questions to which Elroy enthusiastically responds, "Yo".

He has seen too many Sylvester Stallone movies.

The minister then turns to Emma and asks, "Do you take Elroy for your husband, to love and to cherish, to honor, in sickness and in health..... till death do you part?"

Emma says, "Do what?! I thought I just had to know the letters! Wait a minute! This is more than I bargained for!"

And with that runs out of the chapel clutching his letters close to her heart.

Our salvation, life, and happiness do *not* come from the Word but come from Christ who speaks through the Word. Here is my last "for instance" and I will let this go for now. The writer of the twenty-third Psalm talked about the "valley of the shadow of death". There are very few readers who have never experienced that dark valley. You may be reading this and can remember the pain, horror, and loneliness of losing a spouse, parent, or loved one. You may be suffering right now with cancer or AIDS. You may be holding the hand of someone who cannot talk, and you both are wondering why the suffering will not stop.

Have you ever walked through the dark valley? Let me ask you this: What made the difference in that darkness? Was it how much Bible you had memorized? Did you find comfort in reciting the creeds? Did going from Genesis to Revelation and not missing a book pull you through?

For me, when I was walking through the dark night and experiencing the valley of the shadow of death I did not believe anything! You read that right. I did not know what to believe, what to read, what to recite. I felt numb, hurting, and bleeding. What pulled me through was the fact that I had a hand to hold onto. The writer of the twenty-third Psalm said it, "Yeah, though I walk through the valley of the shadow of death, I will fear no evil for *thou art with me*." (Psalm 23:4)

TRADITION

John Wesley offered some very helpful guidelines for deciding the truth. He said look to Scripture first. If it is not in the Word, then it is not of The Truth. After you have found what The Word has to say, let *tradition*, one's *experience*, and *reason* speak to make it relevant and meaningful.

Over the years, I have found Wesley's suggestions very helpful when surrendered to the inspiration of the Holy Spirit. Tradition has been especially helpful in keeping all the modern day religious and spiritual hogwash from watering down the meat and meaning of the Gospel. I am a firm believer in the importance of tradition.

Having said that, and having adequately made an attempt at being diplomatic, I will say this: I will slowly torture the next person who says to me, "We've never done it that way before." There is not enough ink to put to page the number of times the Kingdom of God has been stymied or hindered all for the sake of tradition and "the way we've always done it." It seems, especially in the older established churches, tradition is the god they serve rather than Jesus.

Some of the remarks I have recently heard from various persons in the church I am serving are good examples. They have approached me after the worship service and said, "The Lord really touched me through what you shared. I wanted to say 'Amen', but I didn't think that would be accepted." Likewise, I have had people come up and tell me they felt a real leading to go to the altar, but because it is not the norm -traditionally speaking- for the church, they did not want to go. Well, by goodness!! Let us all worship the way Mr. Stick-In-The-Mud has worshipped for years and forget about being faithful to the response the God of the universe has laid on our hearts. Heaven forbid we shout "Hallelujah" when the love of Jesus is lifted up. Don't you know if you get too excited you will be tossed into eternal flames?! Traditionally, you are supposed to be somber and dignified in worship.

Sarcasm is deeply intended in the previous paragraph.

Obviously the traditionalists have not read the Bible recently. Nowhere is there a record which contains more accounts of the mold being frequently broken than in the New Testament. The Jews thought the Messiah should come with trumpets blasting and armies marching. Surely the Kingdom of God would be ushered in with a BLAST! Untraditionally, God chose to come as a babe and be heralded by stinky shepherds. Traditionally, preachers were supposed to be dignified and upright. John the Baptist broke that mold. Take a gander at the clothes he wore and the cruddy food he ate. He also preached a very undesirable message against the status quo.

And then Jesus came. What does the record show? Untraditionally, Jesus drank, ate, and hung around with the seamy side of humanity. Don't believe me? Take a look at what Jesus says the religious leaders of His day said about Him, "The Son of Man came eating and drinking and they say, 'Here is a drunkard and a glutton; a friend of tax collectors and a sinner.'" (Matthew 11:19)

Then the early church was formed. What next? **Traditionally**, the Jews had been a select bunch. It was inappropriate for them to fraternize with the heathen gentiles. For centuries the Jews stayed away from the Gentiles. Go to the Gentiles? "We've never done it that way!" That is, they had never done it that way until Philip sat in the coach of an Ethiopian Eunuch; Peter listened to the message of a dream and ate with a centurion; and Paul finally became so fed up with the Jew's hardheadedness he became the messenger of Christ's Good News to the Gentiles.

Over and over again the account of the early church states that they broke tradition after tradition. Where would we have been if tradition would have been god-like as it often is today? The answer is actually pretty simple: The church of Jesus Christ never would have made it out of Jerusalem, but would have died as another silly little religious sect.

Tradition is a great springboard from which to jump off into new and exciting areas. Tradition is a wonderful beacon which can call us back if we head off in the wrong direction. But, tradition can also become an easy god to worship because it takes no thought and little energy to "Do it the way we have always done it".

MORALITY

Let's say that hypothetically there is a family in your church who is very moral. As far as any of their family and friends are concerned, they are pillars of the community and have never done a dishonest thing in their lives. Their marriage has lasted for years without even a glimmer of infidelity on the part of either spouse. Let's sweeten the pot even more. Not only are they pillars of the community, but they are also office holders in the church. Not only are they office holders in the church, but they both sing in the choir and give generously to help meet the church's financial needs.

On the surface, you would feel very confident that you are dealing with some "good Christian folk". If you were a minister, and you were faced at some time in the future with conducting their funerals, you would feel assured that they knew Jesus and were standing inside the pearly gates, walking the streets of gold. On what would you base your confident assumption? You would base it on the fact that they were very moral and did all kinds of good deeds.

Now, let us say you happen to be sitting around just "chewing the fat" with this couple when the topic of schools come up. In the midst of a very generic conversation about school curriculum and the like, one of them says in a very matter of fact way, "Well, I'll tell you what I think is wrong with the schools. It's the blacks. You look at any school that's having trouble and you'll find it's full of blacks."

Remember, you just heard this statement shared as if the person were talking about the weather or the quality of house paint.

This "good Christian person" goes on to say, "I guess you ought to know, and I'm not ashamed to say it; I'm a bigot. It's not that I hate blacks. I just think they are the cause of most of our problems and they ought to stay with their kind, and we'll stay with ours."

You finally regain your composure, pick your jaw up off the ground, check your pocket calendar to make sure you have not been transported back to the early 1900's, excuse yourself and go outside and throw up. What is your opinion now? Is this wonderfully moral couple still "good Christian folk" or not?

I have discovered over the years, as I have run into a number of "good Christian folks" just like them, that at an earlier time in their lives, they may very well have *truly* been forgiven for their sins by the blood of Jesus. However, in more instances than not with these people, their relationship with the living, loving Christ stopped right there with that cleansing! They spent the rest of the time playing church, being moral, and remaining satisfied to have their ticket on the soul train to heaven and letting the rest of the world go to hell. Their god has become the lifestyle. Are they still saved? I will let John answer that question:

> "We love because he first loved us. If anyone says, 'I love God,' yet hates his brother, he is a liar. For anyone who does not love his brother, whom he has seen, cannot love God, whom he has not seen. And he has given us this command: Whoever loves God must also love his brother." (I John 4:19-21 NIV)

Morality can be a *sign* that one's life has been turned over to God. Morality, however, is not the means to salvation, nor its proof.

Are any of these false gods keeping you from getting out of the picture and fully immersed in the Spirit of God?

CHAPTER 17

Loosing Control

"I tell you the truth, when you were younger, you dressed yourself and went where you wanted; but when you are old, you will stretch out your hands, and someone else will dress you and lead you where you do not want to go..... then he said to him, 'Follow me!'" (John 21:18 NIV)

Go back and reread that scripture again. In fact, go get your Bible and read all of the twenty-first chapter of the Gospel of John.

The twenty-first chapter is the story of Jesus' appearance to the disciples by the sea. If you remember the story, following his death and resurrection, Jesus had already appeared to the disciples a number of times in Jerusalem. Not long after these appearances, they were sitting in the upper room, contemplating all of the pain, stress, and wonders of the past few days when one of the disciples asked, "Well, what are we going to do now?"

Peter, never wanting for a response, and probably getting a little tired of all the contemplation and prayer said, "I don't know about the rest of you, but I'm going fishing." And off he went.

I am sure that many of the disciples who had been fishermen missed the smells, sights, and sounds of the fishing villages. It may have been therapeutic for Peter and the others to get back to something which was familiar and would hopefully put some stability back in their lives. Whatever the reason for going fishing, they went and soon found themselves out on the water, playing the waiting game with the fish below. John happens to look up and see a fire burning on the shore. He nudges Peter and asks who that person is by their equipment. Peter, being Peter, wants to have a closer look, so he starts rowing back to shore. With every stroke he leans a little further up in his seat and squints his eyes just a little tighter. Suddenly his eyes pop open, he jumps to his feet, and yells, "It's the Lord!"

Before the others in the boat know what is going on, they hear a splash, the boat rocks back and forth, and they see Peter swimming with all of his might toward the stranger on the shore. When they arrive -contrary to popular stuffy church tradition- they had a party! There were hugs, hand shakes, a few slaps on the back, and then Jesus, being Jesus, made sure the essentials were taken care of and offered them a bite to eat. As they all relaxed in the presence of their friend and Savior, Jesus had a personal chat with Peter.

First, Jesus asked Peter three times if Peter truly loved him. There have been a number of books and speculative articles written about why Jesus asked Peter the same question three times. I personally lean in the direction that Jesus was giving Peter a chance to redeem himself and restate his commitment to Christ. Whatever the reason for Jesus asking the same question, with each of Peter's answers, Jesus gave Peter a commission: "Feed my sheep." He was saying to Peter, "I am entrusting to you the glory of sharing the news about me that this dark and hurting world is waiting to hear."

Jesus does not stop with just "Feed my sheep" though. After he makes his remark to Peter for the third time, Jesus adds a little. The little he adds is the opening verse of this chapter. More or less, Jesus is saying to Peter, "All right, if you love me, if you are going to be faithful to me, and take my news to a dark and hungry world, let me spell out for you what you are going to have to go through. You used to call the shots and be the big Mahoona on the beach. No more! In the not so distant future, you will lose control of what happens to you." After Jesus' statement to Peter, the Gospel writer John offers a commentary on Jesus' remarks: "Jesus said this to indicate the kind of death by which Peter would glorify God." (John 21:19 NIV)

Think of how you would feel if you were Peter! Peter had been the big honcho boss man of the beach for years. Jesus had already seen the gift of leadership in Peter. While they were on their way to Jerusalem, Jesus asked the disciples who the people said he was. The disciples readily gave *other's* opinions: "Some say you are a prophet. Some say you are Elijah." Then Jesus asked them, "Who do *you* say I am?"

You can almost see the rest of the disciples looking at one another like a bunch of school kids trying to hide the pet frog they brought to class. It was Peter who stepped forward and in words of calm assurance said, "You are the Christ, the Son of the living God." (Matthew 16:13-16 NIV)

Jesus had seen the gift of leadership and so had given Peter the ultimate opportunity and responsibility. Jesus gave him the keys to the kingdom:

> Jesus replied, "Blessed are you, Simon son of Jonah, for this was not revealed to you by man, but by my Father in heaven. And I tell you that you are Peter, and on this rock I will build my church, and the gates of Hades will not overcome it. I will give you the keys to the kingdom of heaven; whatever you bind on earth will be bound in heaven, and whatever you loose on earth will be loosed in heaven." (Matthew 16:17-19 NIV)

If you were Peter, how would you respond to the Son of God handing you the keys to the Kingdom of Heaven? If you can remember back to the time your father gave you the keys to the family car, you might be able to answer the question with a little more empathy. Remember that night? You had the big date and had just recently acquired your driver's license; that symbol above all symbols which proclaims your independence and approaching adulthood. You walk into the living room where your parents are catching up on the daily news. You go, ever so sheepishly, over to your father and say, "Ddd-dad? Can I take the car out tonight?!"

He looks up from the paper with that "I will kill you and hide the body" look if you scratch his precious car and says, "Do you think you can handle it?"

You enthusiastically say, "Father, my sole desire in life is to fulfill all of your expectations of me and make you and mother proud to have spawned this particular offspring!"

He pretends to have a faint idea of what you have just said, tosses the keys, accompanied by the reminder, "Don't forget to fill it up before you bring it home."

You walk out the door.... how? Do you sneak around the bushes so no one will be able to see you? Do you ask your father to pull the car into the garage so none of your friends will see you get in? NO! You walk out the front door with the keys in your hand, your chest puffed out, a swagger in your step, and your head held high, praying one of your friends will be awed at your new found adulthood!

Peter probably had a similar reaction; "Hey, I'm somebody. I have some authority here." But that is exactly where Peter was wrong. Peter never was in charge. He had only been given *stewardship* of the keys not *ownership*. Before Jesus finally left them bodily, He wanted to make sure Peter had a good grasp of that concept. "Peter, don't misunderstand what is going to happen to you. Because you follow Me, you will not control what happens to you. Don't forget that." (paraphrase of John 21:18)

It was hard for Peter to grasp. It is hard for us to accept. It is also one of the reasons we have such a difficult time with *surrender*. We do not want to turn control over to someone else. The foundation of American pride is that we believe *we* should call all the shots. The ultimate symbol of this innate drive is the little, electronic box which sits on the coffee table next to the recliner in most living rooms. You know that little electronic box as the TV remote!

Take Joe Billings for example. Joe works in the local factory as a repair man. His job is to fix what others have broken. Joe is on call constantly. He might be sitting in his office writing the great American novel, when suddenly his beeper goes off. After a long day of answering these calls, having his day orchestrated and controlled by others, he finally makes it to his last project. This project just happens to be the boss's coffee machine which has been broken since early that morning. You know what happens. The boss launches into a tirade about Joe's incompetence and how he should do a better job of prioritizing. Joe smiles, apologizes, fixes the machine and heads home. Joe walks in the door, falls into his favorite chair, picks up the remote, and a sense of well being and peace flows over his soul. Why? He now has at least a semblance of control over *something*!

One of the real road blocks to reaching God's destination for us is that we want to keep control of at least a little section of our lives so that we will not feel totally out of control. The truth is, however, that it is only when we ultimately relinquish control to God that we truly find the world around us making sense and life becoming more in control.

Remember, the big kid from the playground in chapter two? It is when we give control to God that we finally end up with a life that is truly in control.

Only when He, God, is in control of *everything* will we ever be in control of *anything*.

CHAPTER 18
We're Not Convinced

"When they heard about the resurrection of the dead, some of them sneered, but others said, 'We want to hear you again on this subject.' At that, Paul left the Council. A few men became followers of Paul and believed."
(Acts 17:32-34 NIV)

This story is taken from one of Paul's missionary journeys through the Roman empire. Simply put, Paul was going everywhere his little legs could take him telling people about Jesus. He lands in Athens, the intellectual capitol of the world. In Acts 17:23, Luke says that all of the people of Athens and the foreigners who lived there liked to spend their time discussing ideas and different points of view.

That reminds me of stopping at a convenience store and finding at least a dozen men standing around the coffee machine in the middle of the day solving the world's great dilemmas. There was no coffee machine, but the tradition started in Athens. Paul takes a quick tour around Athens and notices that there is a statue for every god believed to exist at that time. He also notices the people of Athens are thorough. They have a statue with the inscription, "TO AN UNKNOWN GOD".

I guess they wanted to cover all of their bases just in case.

Paul uses this statue to an unknown god as a spring board to tell them about The God who, to that point, was unknown to them. Paul tells them the Gospel of Jesus with all of its grandeur, power, and unbelievable twists. According to Luke, the aspect of the story the Athenians had the most trouble with was the portion about Jesus being resurrected from the dead. The scripture above was Luke's ending to Paul's time in Athens.

Some of the Athenian intellectuals were disgusted. Some were curious..... and *that* was about the extent of their interest. There were a few who believed and went with Paul.

You might be asking yourself what this story has to do with our being reluctant to totally surrender to God. This chapter probably has more to do with our unwillingness to surrender than any other chapter to this point. Try answering the following questions to get a feel for where this is heading:

Why did the people of Athens sneer and become disgusted when Paul talked about a person being resurrected from the dead?

The answer: They did not *believe* it.

Why did most of them remain curious but aloof as far as any real commitment goes?

The answer: They did not fully *believe* it.

Why, out of the thousands in Athens, were there only a handful who followed Paul?

Luke gave the answer: Only a few *believed.*

Do you see a common thread running through each of those answers? The people followed or did not follow Paul; they committed or did not commit to Jesus, depending on whether they believed or did not believe what they were hearing. That gets to the core of why we all are reluctant to fully commit and fully surrender to God. In essence, we are not fully convinced the Gospel is true, and so we hold back if only a little,....just in case we are wrong.

Let's say you live in the Midwest and it is the middle of the summer. You are a grain farmer and there has been a terrible draught for months. Everything everywhere is drying up. People's livelihoods are shriveling and blowing away with each day's new dust storms. Everything your family has worked for generations to build is about to be lost if rain does not come soon.

Is that a bleak enough picture for you?

Along comes a middle-aged, bearded hippie named Isab. Isab has the town gather together for a community meeting. At the meeting, he tells you the good news: If you will give him half of what you currently own, he promises to make it rain. He quotes a number of satisfied customers, and gives you a small demonstration by making it get real humid in the meeting hall. The catch is, there is no guarantee. You will have to take a leap of faith that when you hand over half of your life's savings, he will be able to carry through with his promise and in so doing you will be able to preserve the other half. If it does not rain, you have given him half and there is no way to get it back. What would you do?

Well, what you would do depends a great deal on whether you believe Isab is able to follow through with his promise. If you believe he is, then you enthusiastically give him half because you *know* it is going to save the other half. Half is better than having nothing. If you do not believe him, you are unlikely to make that type of commitment, and simply go on hoping and praying for rain. The key is, do you believe in his promise and his ability to fulfill it.

We *commit* to that which we are *convinced* is real. It is true for farmers, candidates, jobs, spouses, especially in regards to God. Only when we are convinced of the truth do we surrender all.

Take a realistic look at this Gospel of Jesus we are talking about. Let's start off with the fact that God is invisible and no one -at least no one outside of a psychiatric hospital- claims to have seen Him. It is this unseen God who created everything. For the most part, the majority of the people on the planet are at least semi-convinced *some* god exists. Such a complicated world points to an intelligent creator.

Here comes the hard to believe part. This awesome, powerful God decided to create a race with whom He was going to have a relationship. Why? That is another book altogether. Suffice it to say, we have been created and God wants to have a close and abiding relationship with us. The problem is, we do not instinctively want to have a close and abiding relationship with God. Why? Read the previous chapters for a few suggestions. Whatever the reason and whatever the distance we run from God, God continues to seek us out. We spit in God's face, God forgives us. We tell God to get lost, God keeps knocking at the door. Finally, God says "I love you" by becoming human, being born as a little baby, and living among us.

Go back and re-read that last sentence. As you can see, we are getting a little into the bizarre Twilight Zone.

Ah! But the story continues. Even with this wonderful overture of love, we still do not accept God. We trump up false accusations, nail him to a tree, and watch him die in disgrace. He is buried in a borrowed tomb and thought to be gone, but rises from the grave three days later. He appears to a number of his followers and leaves the proof and witness of his resurrection -in fact the entire story- up to a bunch of uneducated and backward fishermen, tax collectors, and prostitutes. A part of the story this rag-tag band have to tell is that if we give all of who we are over to the control of this unseen man, who claims to have been God in the flesh, was killed and then rose again, we would have peace, happiness, joy, and life, now and eternally. We would never die.

See anything in this little recap which might be hard to believe? Honestly speaking, the only thing easy to believe is the part about humans being stubborn. The rest could easily be a matter of opinion.

Why bring this up? Because I am convinced the reason we are so reluctant to surrender all is because most of the Gospel, the Good News of life, *is* so hard to believe. If anything is hard to believe, it is hard to commit to.

I do not think we have a problem believing there is a God. In fact, most surveys show a large percentage of most countries believe there is "some type of supreme being". There is a dramatic difference, however, between believing God exists and having a personal, living relationship with this God based on His unconditional love for us.

Believe it or not, I am not the first person to make this distinction. James stated exactly the same thing when he wrote, "You believe that there is one God. Good! Even the demons believe that---and shudder." (James 2:19)

James is saying that belief in the existence of God is nothing. Even God's enemies know God exists.... and at least *they* react to Him. The question is do you have a *relationship*. Maybe the question is, "Do you believe God wants a relationship *with you*?"

If you are having trouble getting a grip on the difference between knowing someone exists and knowing them personally, think about this analogy. When I was a teen, I had a crush on Susan Anton. Okay, so I was into tall blondes. What can I say. Though I did not know everything about Susan Anton, I did know some of the details about her life and I can guarantee I knew she existed. In fact, the posters on my wall attested to the fact that I knew she existed. Did that mean I knew her? Did my knowing her birth date, favorite color, and her dogs name mean we had a relationship? Not in the least. I never talked with Susan. I never took a stroll by the lake with her at dusk -not that I had not thought about it a few times. I had not even shared a letter with her. She existed and I existed, and that was it. I can still hear my mom say, "So, you believe Susan Anton exists. Good! Even all of her groupies believe she exists and *they* camp outside her house."

If you are currently unwilling to "jump in" because you are not convinced, I would love to be able to convince you. I can tell you what I know. I can hopefully show you a difference in my life. But, when it gets right down to it, you have to step out, surrender all, and let *God* prove it. If He is who He says He is, He will prove it. If He doesn't prove it, then I've wasted my time writing this book, and you're wasting your time reading it.

CHAPTER 19

It Costs Too Much

"Those who had seen it told the people what had happened to the demon-possessed man--and told about the pigs as well. Then the people began to plead with Jesus to leave their region." (Mark 5:16 and 17 NIV)

If there was ever a Bible story that people dance around to avoid the real issue by focusing on the inconsequential details, it is the story of Jesus healing the demon-possessed man who roamed the tombs in the region of Gerasenes.

Here is a quick synopsis of the story. Jesus had just finished astonishing the disciples by calming the storm at sea. After a lengthy period of just staring at Jesus with their mouths wide open, the boat ran aground in the area of Gerasenes. Most likely the disciples thought to themselves, "Oh great! We go from one storm to another." They probably felt this way because they knew about the demon-possessed man who roamed the tombs.

"How did they know?" you ask.

Well, if there was a guy breaking chains, cutting himself with stones, tearing off his clothes, and running around naked terrorizing the area where you fished and hung out, don't you think you would at least have heard a rumor or two?

So, there they were getting out of the boat when low and behold Dr. Deranged comes running out of the tombs ranting and raving something about the Son of God and pointing at their group. Specifically, he was pointing at Jesus. Jesus then makes the supreme mistake and starts talking with the man. Everybody knows the way to handle situations like this is by walking past and hoping the problem will go away on its own. But, Jesus, being Jesus, starts a conversation and the disciples realize this tomb roamer is more dangerous than they thought. He is talking with a number of voices and claims to have more than one spirit in his body. Jesus bargains with the demons about where they will be cast out.

I have always wanted to read someone's opinion on why Jesus even bothered to bargain.

Whatever the reason, Jesus bargained and allowed the demons to go into a herd of pigs. Immediately, the pigs rush over a cliff and drown in the water below. This really isn't that much of an unusual occurrence. Everyone knows that when a herd of pigs suddenly becomes possessed, they immediately rush over a cliff and drown in the water. It is a well documented occurrence.

Can you picture the pig herders? Can you picture introducing your son-in-law as, "Yes, this is my son-in-law... the pig herder?"

There they are, standing at the edge of the cliff looking at all of those damp bacon strips and ham hocks floating in the water. Then they do what any self respecting pig herder would do, they run back and tell their boss. The word gets out that something strange is happening at the tombs. The entire town shows up, finds the dead pigs, and discovers the demon possessed man in his right mind. What do they do?

Did they say, "Wow! This is GREAT! We have been trying to do something with this guy for ages. Jesus, we want you to come to our town and make yourself at home. We'll give you the key to the city and a good home cooked meal!"?

No! They did not.

What did they do? They asked Jesus to leave. They asked him to get out of town!

Think about that! It would be like someone coming to your house and curing your mother of cancer and you respond by throwing the person out. They asked the one who cured this sick man to leave. Why? The answer to that question is a part of why so many are unwilling to fully surrender to God.

The first reason which comes to mind is the price of the pigs. In other words, they ran Jesus off because having him around had already cost them too much *financially*. If this is so, then not only were they putting a price tag on the lost swine, but on the salvation of the demon-possessed man as well.

There is parallel after parallel today with the people of that village. We can see the same attitude in a government whose desire for riches and a posh, comfortable lifestyle are put ahead of other nations' starving and slaugtered thousands. We can see the same shallow perception of value in a city where having clean streets with a welcoming atmosphere is first and foremost; so to create that wonderful atmosphere they run off the homeless and the lost instead of helping them. We can see the same attitude in communities which hide behind pretty homes and allow one more child to become a victim of abuse. We can see it in churches which gold plate their pews and allow hundreds in their own back yard to die without ever hearing the Gospel of Jesus.

You can almost hear the townspeople saying, "Jesus, do you know how much you cost us? We can't afford this. I have college, braces, mortgage, and new chariot payments. Go bother some other city." They drove him away because he cost too much.

Maybe they drove Jesus away because they *did not understand* what was going on. They just were not used to this type of thing. Or, maybe they fully understood and wanted no part of it. These people were probably pretty comfortable with a nice, static, meaningless religion which never shook the status quo, and which allowed them to go their merry way without much confusion or disruption. All of a sudden, here comes this boat-rocking, demon-casting, pig killer. His actions and message have meaning and power. He calls for transformation and results..... commitment. You can almost hear them say, "For years we have satisfied ourselves to simply list this naked cemetery walker in our church bulletin prayer list. Every Christmas and Thanksgiving we draw straws to see who is going to take the 'Meal on Donkeys' out to the cemetery to feed this pour soul. Jesus, what did you go and do something so radical for?!"

They saw a difference in this man from their sad, shallow religion and they wanted to get rid of the reminder. They knew Jesus was calling them beyond their safe mediocrity. This man walked with power and conviction! What he said made a difference. What he said *worked*!

They looked at his clothes and saw they were not adorned with silk and jewels. He did not offer riches. They looked at his friends and saw a bunch of uneducated, rag-tag fishermen, prostitutes, and sinners. He did not offer prestige. They had probably already heard him talk about crosses to bear and tribulations to face. He dealt with demon-possessed people. He talked about, lived, and enabled change and growth!

Can you hear them? "Thank you. No. We are quite content. We do not really want to pay the price. Hey! Jesus, don't think badly of us. It's not like we've killed anyone or anything." And with his departure their souls died a little more.

Many times we never get over the wall because in our minds, full surrender to God costs too much for our comfortable life-style. So, we pick another side road that is easier and more comfortable and turn a deaf ear to God's call to walk the right road to His perfect destination.

CHAPTER 20
It's Not Possible

"Be perfect, therefore, even as your heavenly father is perfect." (Matthew 5:48 NIV)

Perfection. It is a controversial term to say the least. On the one hand, society in general almost always expects it. There are the parents who want their child to be the best in the class. If little Suzy Que brings home a report card with all A's and one B, Dad will look over the card and not say a word. Then, as he is handing it back to her, he will look her in the eye with an expression of suspicion -or worse, disappointment- and ask, "Why not all A's?"

Honestly speaking, in my house, while I was in grade school, if I would have brought home a report card with all C's and one B, my mother would have called the newspapers and my dad would have written "Ripley's Believe It Or Not"!

Perfection. We expect it from our athletes. On a nationally televised gymnastics competition a few years ago, young girls ranging from 12 to 18 years of age were tumbling and twisting their bodies in ways I have only done after falling in the campfire at "Camp Wanna Be A Big Man". Some of the moves these "frail" little girls were making were unbelievable. Not only were they making them in their tumbling exercises, but they were doing them on a four inch wide piece of wood, four feet off the ground while swinging between two bars sadistically set at different heights to more likely insure injury. During the entire performance my girls and I were marveling at their skill.

It was not long into the third or fourth routine when one of the announcers started his "commentary" on what we, the awe struck audience, were viewing. He decided to bless us with his wonderful years of wisdom and experience by pointing

159

out every little flaw, bobble, and mistake made by every gymnast. The young girl would accidentally bat her eye and the commentator would say, "Ah, see Frank, she has had a momentary lapse in concentration. That will definitely be a deduction of .01."

Another young lady would do a triple axle flip with a double somersault ending with her playing the Hallelujah chorus on a grand piano as she dismounted from the uneven bars. On the landing, her foot would scoot about an inch in order to -you will not believe this- regain her balance, and our gifted commentator would say, "Oh! I really wish she could have stuck that landing. If only she had more time to spend on her routine instead of volunteering for the Peace Corps and trying to make decent grades. Kids today really need to get their priorities straight. That will be a point one deduction." A point one deduction for a one inch slide of the foot. I would be happy just to land on my feet without dislocating some important portion of my body.

Perfection. It has become the standard by which society measures everything.

On the other hand, while society likes perfection, many I have encountered in *religious* circles seem to have a real problem talking about perfection; wanting to work toward perfection, and an absolute disgust for those who may claim to have obtained perfection. I know this because of the number of conversations I have had since I began sharing my picture and its implications.

The conversation almost always goes like this: I would share my picture, a brief sketch of its implications, and then end with something like, "I believe this is God's goal and desire for our lives. That we would be fully, totally, and completely surrendered to Him; that His Spirit would be completely in us, so that when others see us, they see Him."

One of the more frequent responses is, "WHAT!? You're talking about perfection. The only person who was ever perfect and had God's presence completely in him was Jesus! What you are saying is very unbiblical!"

"Unbiblical? What then do you consider to be the Biblical truth?", I ask.

The scripture most often quoted in response to that has been Romans 3:23 where Paul says, "We all have sinned and fallen short of the glory of God."

I usually respond, "I'm not disagreeing with that. We *have* all sinned and we all *do* fall short of God's glory and plan. God's plan is for us to be fully surrendered and radiating His presence. It is *that plan* which we fall short of."

After a few minutes of "excited" discussion, I always like to throw out the scripture that began this chapter: "Be perfect, therefore, as your heavenly father is perfect." (Matthew 5:48). Once I have allowed that particular scripture to sink in within the context of my picture, I usually try to address their concerns by saying something like, "Let me say that this is not something which is easily obtained. I have to admit -personally speaking- that I have never met a person who day in and day out is completely surrendered and filled with the Spirit of God. I would never make that claim for myself. Even John Wesley, who also talked about Christian Perfection -being made perfect in God's love- said he had never met a perfect Christian. But, that does not undo the fact that it is still the goal of the Christian faith: For us to be fully absorbed in the person, presence, and Spirit of the Living God."

So far, without one single exception, someone will say in response to my remarks something like, "What about Paul. I think Paul would be the closest person to what you are talking about and he never claimed to be perfect."

I smile, take a quick look up to heaven to thank God for opening the door again and say, "No, but he talked about working towards it. He said, 'Not that I have already obtained all this, or have already been made *perfect*, but I press on to

take hold of that for which Christ Jesus took hold of me.'"
(Philippians 3:12 NIV)

I would love to say that at that point in the conversation everyone's struggles, troubles, and questions have been resolved with the sharing of that scripture. Alas, that is usually not the case. Many people have a real, and apparently permanent problem with the idea of perfection in Christ. The question that needs to be answered here is "Why?" Why do so many people have a problem with the concept of being perfect in God?

Arrogance

From what I have gathered, the first thing which crosses people's minds and which raises red flags about the concept of perfection, is how arrogant it sounds. To many people, even the belief that humanity can pursue perfection is so arrogant it borders on foolishness. Admittedly, it is a rather arrogant sounding statement. I have never gotten a real thrill out of being around people who considered themselves the world's answer to anything. There is nothing more nauseating than to hear an interview with an athlete who thinks he is the "cat's meow" at his particular sport and that there is no other athlete of his or her stature. True arrogance is repulsive and ungodly. But is arrogance the right word to use in this particular case?

An arrogant person is one who thinks more highly of himself than he ought. Not only does he think too much of himself, but an arrogant person spends a great deal of time telling others about how wonderful he is. The perfection Jesus was talking about, however, and set before us as our destination is quite the opposite. One's ability or receptivity to moving in the direction of perfection in God is dependent on one first realizing one's *inadequacies*. Completely opposed to arrogance is the statement made by someone working towards Godly perfection, "I realize I am incomplete in myself. What will make me whole is to wholly -or "holy"- get rid of the me

162

and belong to God." In this respect, our "pressing on" toward perfection is anything *but* arrogant.

Whether you still consider the idea arrogant or not, you have to admit that this would not be the first time a truth of God has been described as foolish:

> "For the message of the cross is foolishness to those who are perishing but to us who are being saved, it is the power of God..... Has not God made foolish the wisdom of the world? For since in the wisdom of God the world through its wisdom did not know him, God was pleased through the foolishness of what was preached to save those who believe..... we preach Christ crucified: a stumbling block to Jews and foolishness to Gentiles,.... For the foolishness of God is wiser than man's wisdom, and the weakness of God is stronger than man's strength." (I Corinthians 1:18-25 NIV)

Other's Expectations

Let's say a person can get beyond the perceptions of arrogance and foolishness and admit, maybe even proclaim, he is -like Paul- moving onto perfection and being completely surrendered in the Spirit. The next fear which immediately comes to my mind is: What then will be other people's expectations of my lifestyle? What I mean is, if I claim to be aware of where God is calling me, if I claim to be moving in that direction, and if I claim that I am being filled with God's Spirit, won't others have greater expectations of what my Christian witness should be? The answer to that is a resounding, "YES!" In fact, not only will there be greater expectations, but many people -some possibly right within your own family- will be waiting for you to slip up so they can point a nice condemning finger at your mistakes, emphasize your lack of growth, and say mature things like, "I told you so! I told you so! Nyahh Nyahhnee boo-boo!!"

I know that sounds a little paranoid. Take my word for it. It happens. I've seen it happen in church after church. I've seen it happen especially with new believers.

163

Think about Fred Almond. You mean you don't know who Fred Almond is? Pull up a chair and let me fill you in. Fred Almond is known around town as a lazy free loader. He can barely hold a job for a month before his boss realizes the company is loosing money and that Fred has been ripping them off. Fred has a shaky marriage, obnoxious kids, and goes to church on Christmas and Easter to appease his mother.

One day, Fred finally opens his heart and experiences new life in Jesus Christ. His entire outlook on life changes. Because of his desire to respond to Christ's wonderful gift of grace, Fred dedicates every day to making Jesus proud of him. He gets a new job. He starts attending marriage counseling with his wife, and begins to rebuild the bridge with his kids. He also starts attending church regularly, sitting next to his beaming, gray haired mother.

Close your eyes. Picture yourself in the pews about three rows back from Fred and his family. You are sitting next to Aunt Matilda and Ruthy Mae. What do you hear? Probably something like this:

"Well, it won't last."

"Once a bum always a bum!"

"He probably just wants some money from his mother or his wife finally threatened to leave him. Give it a few more weeks and he'll be back to his old ways."

"Why, I remember when......."

Sound familiar? It should. You may have even been an Aunt Matilda or a Ruthy Mae at some time. I have said a number of times from the pulpit that one of the worst places for a new Christian is the church. The reason for that is, when someone claims to be working toward a deeper surrender and relationship with God, many shallow, "need a life", religious, pew-sitters perch like vultures waiting for the fall. Why? People feel better about their own lack of growth when they see others apparently fail.

Face To Face

Another problem people have with the idea of their own perfect surrender is though we like to *talk* about God as "My best bud," we still like to keep a little distance between us and God. Don't agree? Do you think the answer to your prayers would be to have God stand at the base of your bed in a glowing cloud and "chat" the night away? Take a few hours to read over the accounts in the Bible where people *did* stand in the presence of God. Without many exceptions, they were terrified! Moses was a bit rattled when he heard God speaking through the burning bush. The people at Sinai didn't even want to approach the mountain because they were terrified when they saw the cloud of the Lord. Isaiah was brought to his knees when he saw God's glory in the temple. Over and over again, those who have stood in the unparalleled brightness of God have fallen on their knees and have wished for a little bit of separation.

I am not saying that being in the presence of God is not something I long for every morning when I start my daily devotions. On the contrary, when I can feel His gentle touch, my day truly begins and life is started in my heart. My daily devotional time, however, is like experiencing God through a filter. Quoting Paul, "Now we see but a poor reflection as in a mirror; then we shall see face to face." (I Corinthians 13:12 NIV) I'm not sure how I would handle it if that filter were completely removed.

Think of it this way: Wouldn't you love to have a conversation with the President of the United States. Wouldn't you like to talk to him about social issues and world problems, to find out about his faith and what he really believes about Jesus, rather than what he says during an election year. Imagine an appointment has been made and tomorrow is the day. It has gone from a letter, to a phone call, and now the face to face meeting is about to happen. You have been briefed by the secret service and are just about to walk into the oval office. What do you do? Throw up! At least I probably would. Not only would I throw up, but I would probably want to get back to the safe confines of a phone call. That face to face stuff can be rather threatening.

Perfect surrender moves us very, very close to face to face.... or at least spirit to Spirit.

Change

Lastly, many have a problem with the concept of perfect surrender because we are afraid of what might be asked of us if we *do* move further in that direction and are lead completely by the Spirit of God. Your life will indeed change. Change and challenge are not always the most enticing things to people who live in a society which values security and position.

Whatever the argument or disagreement, we cannot pick and choose the portions of God's word we want to deal with. I think, especially with this topic, Samuel Clemmons was right when he said, "It is not the scriptures I *don't* understand that give me the most trouble. Rather, the one's I *do*."

Jesus said, "Be perfect, therefore, as your heavenly father is perfect." (Matthew 5:48)

Tear down the wall and open up your soul to the inspiration and the "full-filling" of God's Holy Spirit.

Now What?

"Thomas said to him, 'Lord, we don't know where you are going, so how can we know the way?'"(John 14:5)

Hopefully, by this point, you are anxiously wondering, "How? How do I begin to move toward what has been described in this book?"

"How do I get beyond all that I have been taught throughout my life and begin to see all the wonders and glories God has in store for me?

"How do I make myself available, and open my heart, mind, and soul to be filled with God's Spirit?"

Are any of those questions running around in your cerebral cortex? Are you biting at the bit, so to speak, to start down the marvelous path God has in store? Great! That has been my constant prayer throughout the writing of this book, that those who would read the thoughts on these pages would become excited about growing deeper in their relationship with God.

One of my pet peeves about preaching is when those listening are only intellectually challenged. Though it is nice to have people leave a service and say, "You gave me something to think about today, Preacher," it is thrilling to have someone grab my hand, tears in her eyes, and say, "How? How do I get what you were talking about?"

I hope you are to that point. I hope the Holy Spirit has not only been *speaking* to your mind throughout this book, but *exciting* your soul as well. If you are not to the point of asking "How?", go back and read the book again. Trust me, you will thank me later.

If you are to the "How?" stage, now what? How do we move deeper and closer to being out of the picture, to becoming immersed in the presence and Spirit of God?

In this section I am going to share some "suggestions". These suggestions are scripturally based. They have been verified through Christian history, and they make perfect sense. But the primary measuring rod for what you will find in this section is my experience. I am using my experience because I simply want to give a witness to what I know to be some of the answers to "How?"

How, then, do we become immersed in the Spirit of God and get out of the picture as we move forward and deeper in our relationship with God?

CHAPTER 21

Know the truth

"You shall know the truth, and the truth shall set you free"
(John 8:32   NIV)

The first step in having all that this book has covered become real in your life, is to *know* that this is truly God's design and desire for your life. Notice I did not say, "First *think* about this being God's design," or " Be partially convinced...." I said, "KNOW!"

Know the truth that God created each of us, and wants to be in a relationship with us.

Know the truth that we are constantly turning away -it is our nature- and the chasm between us and God becomes bigger and bigger.

Know the truth; that Jesus died so we could receive salvation by faith. He died to bridge the gap which separates us from God, and to enable us to walk into God's presence. In so doing, Jesus has made available a living relationship with God.

Know that every scripture which speaks of God's *ultimate will* for your life is referring to your being immersed in His Spirit.

Know that when Paul wrote Romans, Chapter 8, verse 28: "We know that all things work together for good for those who love God, who are called according to his purpose," the "purpose" Paul was referring to was our getting out of the picture and becoming immersed.

"You shall **know** the truth and the truth shall set you free!"

Do you know this truth? Has it gone beyond just an intellectual exercise or some interesting insight you might be able to preach the next time the minister is out of the pulpit?

Do *you* know this truth? Knowing it is the first step in this truth setting you free.

Wait a minute! Why all this emphasis on knowing? That sounds a little like suggesting we have to "understand" this truth before it becomes a reality in our lives. Hardly! I am only just beginning to get a glimpse of the tip of the iceberg in *understanding* the truths I have shared in this book. As the prophet Isaiah said, "God's ways are not our ways." (Isaiah 55:8) Understanding has nothing to do with it. In fact, if you have a complete understanding of God's ways, I would bet good money that you have the wrong god.

Does "knowing" have to do with being convinced? Not the *knowing* I am talking about at this point. There is a point at which we are going to need enough faith that we take a step of faith in God's direction whether we can see solid ground below us or not. But being *convinced*, or having a certain level of faith, is not the starting point. Don't make it too complicated. "Know" means to "know", as opposed to "I did not know".

Think of the Ephesians. When Paul met the members of the church at Ephesus, he asked them, "Did you receive the Holy Spirit when you believed?"

They responded, "We have not even heard that there was a Holy Spirit." (Acts 19:1-3) Their problem was not understanding or lack of faith. It was that they had not even been informed.

One of the frightening things I run into in every church I have ever served is the number of people who have never been told that God has more in store for them than just getting their soul saved, their sins forgiven, and their ticket on the soul train to heaven. They simply do not *know* -because they have not heard- that there is a Holy Spirit.

First, know the truth which will truly set you free.

Of course, by the time you have gotten to this point in the book, step number one is completed.

Hey! That means you are on your way! Take a minute to celebrate! Life is about to take off for you in ways you have never imagined!

Know that it's a Process

Know that this filling, this deepening relationship is a *process*.

In Matthew 4:18-21 Jesus is taking a nice, leisurely stroll by the sea and spots Peter and Andrew hard at work. He walks up and offers the now famous invitation, "Follow me and I will make you fishers of men." I firmly believe that if Peter and Andrew would have been a part of one of the prominent denominations of today, their response would probably have been, "Well, Lord, we appreciate the offer. You know we have a lot of things going on in our lives right now. Tell you what, give us a few days. We'll set up a committee to examine the feasibility of following you, and get back to you as soon as we can."

That, of course, was not their response! How *did* they respond? Did they look at each other in bewilderment and awe, smile broadly and say, "He wants us! Can you believe it! This miracle working teacher wants us to follow him! What a privilege! We can die happy and fulfilled now!" and then go back to what they were doing? No way! Jesus had not made them an offer to buy a postcard of a cruise liner and simply celebrate their being invited. Jesus wanted them to take a *journey* with Him!

Read that again: Jesus wanted Peter and Andrew to take a *journey with Him*. If that is the case, was Jesus' calling of these two unlikely candidates the beginning or the end of their journey? There is no question: It was the beginning. Oh Buddy, was it the beginning! They had so much ahead of them that if Jesus had given them even a part of the complete picture, they would have passed out from sheer exhaustion. The point is this: When we finally hear Christ's knock at the door, when we finally respond to his call, our initial response is not the destination but the *start* of a journey. Jesus wants us to get up from our altar of conversion and go forward in our relationship with Him! To say it succinctly: Our salvation experience is the beginning of the process, not the end.

Please note one of *the* operative words used throughout this book: **Relationship**. Simply put, Jesus makes available a relationship with God that is worked out in a journey. Understanding this concept of relationship is one of the major stumbling blocks for Christians moving deeper in their faith. Most people -Christians and non-Christians alike- believe that Christianity is a one time ticket we purchase. They believe that we simply go into the "soul train" station, complete the required transaction, and leave with our ticket. But, Christianity -salvation- is not a completed transaction. It is a living, hopefully growing relationship. It is a relationship that we either choose to nurture and work on, or walk away from.

Marriage is a good parallel. As my father used to say, "When two people are about to get married, they have absolutely no idea what they are getting themselves into." When that couple says, "I do," on their blissful wedding day, is that the end or the beginning of the marriage? Granted, it is the end of the ceremony, and they are officially married. But is the work of being married over or just beginning? The answer is a resounding: "JUST BEGINNING!" The easy part is getting married. A couple stands up in front of a preacher, repeats a few words, tries not to pass out, looks googly-eyed at each other, has a party afterward, and then takes an expensive trip. The real work *starts* when they get back from their expensive trip and get down to the business of building a relationship.

Paul wrote to the church at Phillipi:

"Not that I have already obtained this or have already reached the goal: but I **press on** to make it my own, because Christ Jesus has made me his own. Beloved, I do not consider that I have made it my own; but this one thing I do: forgetting what lies behind and straining forward to what lies ahead, I **press on** toward the goal....." (Phillipians 3:12-14a) (bold print added for emphasis)

Keep in mind that this is *Paul* writing to the church at Phillipi. I think we can all agree that Paul was a pretty saintly guy. He may have had a flaw here or there, but there are few people in history who have been filled with the Spirit of God as obviously as Paul. Yet Paul, when talking about full and complete surrender of the heart and soul to God, wrote these words, "....not that I have already obtained this, or have already been made perfect, but I *press on....*"

"Not that I have already obtained this or have already been made perfect, but I *press on*."

Read it again. Paul is saying that he hasn't reached the ultimate goal of getting out of the picture yet. He knows it is out there. He knows that he is making progress toward it; that slowly, more and more of God's Spirit is taking up residence in his heart. But there is still the need to keep "pressing on". It is a life long, time consuming process!

A number of years ago, I heard another mental picture which helps communicate the whole "process" idea of God's desire for our lives.

Picture a house. Not just any house. The house of your life. It's the Beverly Hillbilly's house. Everywhere you look there are rooms, windows, and closets galore. When we first give our lives to Christ, we open the front door and let Him in. Now that He's in, we might as well give Him the key to the front door. Done. Now what? Well, too many of us just pull up a chair for our guest right there in the hallway, and tell him to make himself at home while we go about the rest of our business..... alone. The only problem is the knocking doesn't stop. Our responding might end, but the knocking on all the remaining doors inside our house persists. Remember, this is a mansion. This mansion holds everything you are. For every room, there's a door. For every door, there's a key..... and God wants access to *all* of them. So.... He knocks.

173

Maybe the first door is to your Sunday morning activities. You have just recently allowed him in the front door and he graciously helped clean up the mess on the front porch. Not only has he helped you clean up the front porch, but he has worked a miracle by straightening up the foyer. The least you can do is give him a few hours on Sunday morning. You hand over the key to the Sunday morning activity room without a great deal of fuss.

Maybe the next room is your language room. Though you have always thought of yourself as pretty tough because of your foul mouth, you know Jesus isn't going to like that type of language in his presence. He has promised to help you clean that room as well, so you break down again and give him the key to your language room.

He has made his way through the living room, dining room, and maybe even your work room. Some of the keys have been easier than others to give up. Now he's standing at the door to your entertainment closet. Or maybe it's your closet of self image, or popularity, or security. For this illustration *you* pick the room he is standing before. You know the room I'm talking about. It's the room whose key you are holding tight with a white knuckled grip. It's the last place you would want Jesus "interfering". There you both stand. He's knocking. You're fidgeting. Finally, you put your hand back over the glass and say, "Sorry. Stop pouring. No more keys for now. This is as far as I can go."

What does Jesus do? Remember, we are talking about grace. It is patient, understanding, free, and most of all it does not force itself on you. What does Jesus do? He waits. He keeps knocking, but he waits until..... until you are ready to move on.

It is a process.

"Not that I have obtained all of this or have already been made perfect, but I **press on** toward the goal......"

The point is, just like exercise -or *any* growth- **holiness is a process**. There will be times when great strides are made up the hill. One day will be dramatically different from the day before. Because of circumstances or insights, you will make huge leaps forward and feel a renewed bond between yourself and God's Spirit. Then three days later you may hit a brick wall -just like in exercising- where you don't make *any* progress and even slip back a notch or two. The thing to remember is that it *is* a process. It *will* take time. There will be ups. There will be downs. There will be gorgeous peaks with wondrous vistas....and there will be plateaus with swamp water and bugs. The key? Paul said it, "I press on toward the goal..." (Phillipians 3:14 NIV)

CHAPTER 22
Set Sail

"When he had finished speaking, he said to Simon, 'Put out into deep water, and let down the nets for a catch.'"
(Luke 5:4 NIV)

About a year ago, I heard the song "Set Sail" by Ray Boltz. At first, I simply enjoyed the uplifting beat and tempo of the song. It wasn't until about the third time I listened to the song that the words began to sink through my dense skull. Here is an excerpt from that song:

> "Set sail! The Captain's calling. It's time to climb aboard.
> Set sail. There's room for all and there's such a great reward.
> There's not a chance you can fail. Set sail!"

"Set sail"......   "Set sail!"   The words have been a haunting chant in my head ever since they finally sank in. "Set sail! The Captain's calling. It's time to climb aboard! Set sail." These words have haunted me for so long, first of all, because God has been saying through these words, "Jim, there are places I want you to go. There are things I want you to do. There are oceans which need to be crossed in order to accomplish the work I have ready for you."

These words have haunted me, secondly, because God has been saying to a number of persons in the church I serve, "Untie the mooring lines! Push away from the safety of the docks and set out into the deep. Go where you never thought you would ever be able to go."

Finally, I believe these words have haunted me because as I have been writing this book, I have come to realize more and more that the call to "set sail" is Christ's constant call to *every* committed believer. If we listen, we would hear Jesus clearly saying, "Set sail! Don't lie around tanning yourself on the beach, dangling your feet in the water thinking 'happy thoughts'. If you know the Captain, get on board and ride!"

I don't know what scripture motivated Ray Boltz to write this song. But I would not be surprised if it was the fifth chapter of Luke. "Set Sail!" That is exactly what Jesus was saying to Simon -Peter.

Just before the account in Luke 5, Luke has shared a few of Christ's wonderful miracles and works. He recounts some of the healings which Jesus performed, and writes about the rejection of Jesus on the part of some of the religious leaders because of His Good News being too status-quo shaking. Finally, Luke states that because of what had been seen and heard, great crowds followed Jesus everywhere he went.

There were probably as many reasons for following Jesus as there were people in the crowd. Some probably followed him out of curiosity. They were thinking to themselves, "Who is this strange man who speaks with authority and confounds the religious leaders?"

Some probably followed because of greed. In their heart of hearts, they were thinking, "I need or I want something. Maybe Jesus is the person who can supply it."

Others surely followed Jesus out of despair. They literally had no one or nowhere else to turn. And, of course, there were the few who followed Jesus because of a pure and honest commitment. They believed Jesus was who he said he was, and they wanted to have the life Jesus promised. Whatever the legion of reasons, the people followed Jesus this particular day until there were so many surrounding Jesus that he was being pushed off the shore and into the water.

Now hold that picture for just a minute. Imagine this huge crowd of people. There are people of different ages, sexes, and tribes; all there with different motives and agenda; all wanting to get a little piece of the carpenter from Nazareth. All of them staring in amazement and curiosity as Jesus shares truths and insights most of them had never heard before. He taught. They listened.

But! if you bother to read the rest of the Gospels and their accounts of what these same "attentive" listeners and "starers" did, and did *not* do, they obviously were not *hearing* much of what Jesus was saying. It was not too long after this lesson by the sea shore, when the going got a little tough and the call for commitment sounded a little too close to home, that many of those present simply walked away.

You can almost see Jesus standing there. It is an unusual picture in the first place; a man, teaching from a boat to a huge crowd gathered on the shore. If you close your eyes, you can see Jesus pause. He is aware that many of the people are there simply to be entertained. He knows the truths he has been sharing have been falling on either deaf or very distracted ears. He pauses, and the scene grows deathly quiet. The sudden silence knocks the people back on track. Jesus, still silent, simply looks over the now attentive crowd. The only noise you hear is the lapping of the waves against the shore and the periodic whine of a little baby. Jesus looks over the crowd and starts to catch people's eyes. He looks right past the facades and sees deep into their souls. In some, he sees hunger and thirst for truth. He knows they are hanging onto his every word, longing for something to give them hope. In others, he sees nothing but blank expressions, and knows his words are penetrating about as well as a tennis ball through a brick wall. Then Jesus turns toward Peter and the others in the boat. They have stopped washing their nets just long enough to see what the quietness is all about. Jesus looks directly into Peter's eyes and says, "Go out into the deep water."

At this Peter's eyes bug out of his head. You can sense that he wants to get a little closer to Jesus and in a street wise whisper say, "Listen teacher, I know you're supposed to be smart and all, but going out into the deep is not a good thing right now. You've got them right where you want them. This is a captive audience. Don't blow it." He probably thinks it, but doesn't say it. Then, what Jesus asked him to do really starts to sink in. Peter squints his eyes as he reruns the tape in his head of what Jesus had just said. "What did he say to me?" Peter asks himself. "Go out into the deep and do what?" Then his eyes bug even further out of their sockets as he remembers the last part of Jesus' "suggestion". He sits up to his full sitting height, puffs out his chest, and desperately wants to say, "What?! You want me to do what? Let down my nets? Are you crazy?"

But even outspoken Peter can't be that disrespectful. He has to say something though. He manages this: "Master, we've worked hard all night and haven't caught anything." (Luke 5:5a)

Try and get under Peter's skin here and get a feel for what is going on. Think of all of the things running through Peter's mind during this exchange. First of all, Peter is *tired*. He has worked hard all night. It's time to go to the Quick Stop and have a soda with the boys. Being inconvenienced is not his number one goal at the moment. It is much more comfortable on the shore.

Peter is probably *confused*. Jesus apparently has the crowd hanging on his every word. Why in the world would Jesus want to leave this crowd to go off and do something which not only was inconvenient, but did not make a lot of sense.

Most likely Peter was a little *insulted*. Who is this carpenter from Nowheresville telling Peter, the master of all fisherpersons, how to do his job?! You can almost hear Peter saying, "Listen Jesus, you stick with pegs and wood shavings and I'll do what the school of hard knocks has taught me."

Over and over Peter runs through the logical reasons why they should *all* stay on the shore: It's more comfortable. It doesn't make sense. I know what is best for me. And as Peter has his inner debate and for once manages to hold his tongue, Jesus just stands there with a slight, knowing smile on his face. No extra response to Peter. Jesus doesn't repeat the call vocally. Once was enough. Now Peter is looking into Jesus' eyes, and those soul piercing eyes are saying with renewed emphasis, "Peter, trust me. Go out into the deep."

Please note Peter's final response. We tend to pick on Peter's lack of faith and his constant bungling because it helps us feel better about our own shortcomings. But here Peter sees something in those eyes which says, "Trust me. Do what I say." Peter responds, "But because you say so, I will let down the nets." (Luke 5:5b NIV)

Though there is admittedly some faith demonstrated here and *some* obedience on the part of Peter, this is a prime example of faith "the size of a mustard seed." Peter did not say, "Ah! I see your plan! I understand your reasons and because I know you are great and mighty, I will surrender all to you." Rather, Peter said -probably with a long, drawn out sigh- "All right. All right. There's something about you. I'll do it. I don't like it. I don't want to, and it doesn't make sense, but I'll do it." Peter reluctantly leaves the shore, pushing out into the deep, and sets sail with the Captain. The result? They catch more fish than any of them could possibly imagine. Here is how Luke described what occurred:

> "When they had done so, they caught such a large number of fish that their nets began to break. So they signaled their partners in the other boat to come and help them, and they came and filled both boats so full that they began to sink." (Luke 5:6,7 NIV)

Can you hear them laughing and "whooping it up?" Can you see them nudging each other, denarii signs flashing in their eyes as they think about all that they are going to be able to buy with this great catch. One or two of them say to the others, "This is wonderful! A few more catches like this and we can retire!" It's a party at sea!

So, what's the point? Why *did* Jesus ask Peter to push out into the deep and do a little extracurricular fishing? Was

Jesus trying to say to them, "Stick with me kids, you'll go places. With me, everything you do is going to be successful! You will have two chariots in every garage. Your business will boom. Your church will grow. You will have the 'Midas touch' and everything you contact will be turned to gold!"

Maybe the crowds needed a little extra incentive to follow him, so he decided to show them that they could benefit financially. It's possible that Jesus was trying to "bribe" the people into following him. There are obviously enough preachers today who believe we can be bribed into committing our lives to Christ. What other reason would there be for so many to promise riches, prosperity, and worldly bliss if a person would surrender to Jesus? There has to be some reason for the rampant preaching of the "Gospel of Prosperity." It certainly is not because that teaching is found in the Bible.

Was Jesus trying to bribe the crowds? Hardly. Verses eight through ten show that hard headed Peter got the message:

> "When Simon Peter saw this, he fell at Jesus' knees and said, 'Go away from me, Lord; I am a sinful man!' For he and all his companions were astonished at the catch of fish they had taken, and so were James and John, the sons of Zebedee, Simon's partners." (Luke 5:8-10 NIV)

What was the message for them, and what *is* the point for us today? How does this story answer the question of *how* one begins to be fully surrendered and immersed in the Spirit of God? Simple, if we want God's Spirit to permeate our pores, if we're wanting to move in the direction of being out of the picture, then we must push away from the dock and set sail with The Captain.

Look at the three lessons Peter learned when he reluctantly pushed out into the deep.

First of all, Peter came to know **who Jesus was**. Once Peter came to his senses and paused long enough to think beyond the financial rewards, he looked at Jesus, fell at Jesus' feet and said, "Go away from me, LORD...."

I know from personal experience that Bible studies, prayer and exposing oneself to Christian teachings is vitally important to one's relationship with God. It is in doing and experiencing these that a foundation of truth is laid. Luke points out, "Jesus was standing by the lake of Gennesaret, with the people crowding around him and listening to the word of God." (Luke 5:1) However, if we want to *know* the Lord, if we want to be convinced of who he is; to be assured that he *is* the one who rules the wind, he *is* the one who overcomes the world, it will only happen when we get off the shore and get out into the deep water to where he is calling us. Jesus was saying to Peter, "Push out into the deep because I want you to know who I am."

Secondly, out in the deep, Peter began to know that **anything was possible**. We love to quote Paul's words in Phillipians where he says, "I can do all things through Christ who gives me strength." (Phillipians 4:13) We say these words and feel very religious about ourselves. But do we really know the truth of what Paul is saying?

Paul did not write those powerful words after years of Bible study in the safe confines of his Jewish synagogue. That marvelous insight did not dawn on Paul one evening while he was dining at a fellowship dinner with the Pharisees. Read what Paul writes just prior to the thirteenth verse:

> "I know what it is to be in need, and I know what
> it is to have plenty. I have learned the secret of
> being content in any and every situation, whether
> well fed or hungry, whether living in plenty or in
> want. I can....." (Phillipians 4:12 NIV)

Do those sound like the words of someone who is lounging around playing freeze tag on the shore? NO! Those are the words of someone who has been in the trenches and out in the deep. Those are the words of someone who has not had to wait for someone to come back to shore and tell them what's going on out in the deep. He was there. He was there because he followed the Captain's call to push out in the direction the Captain pointed. He saw *first hand* what The Captain could do. Jesus was saying to Peter, "Push out into the deep and let me *show you* what's possible."

Thirdly, Peter began to **know himself**. Read again Peter's words, "Go away from me Lord; I am a sinful man!" (Luke 5:8   NIV)

Peter did not say this while he was sitting on the shore. This realization of who he was came crashing in on him when he pushed out in the deep and was in "way over his head." We need to experience the same thing. As long as we stay in the shallows and simply play religion, we will consider ourselves very self-sufficient and people of "fine moral character." What else would we consider ourselves if we are disciplined enough to attend church once a week. "I'm not all that bad," we keep reminding ourselves. "My neighbor, Joe, never goes to church." we say. "At least I show up every once in awhile. That's more than I can say for a lot of people."

That attitude about ourselves is a far cry from, "I am a sinful man!"

Why do we need to be out in the deep in order to realize our inadequacies? Simply put, it's out there that we *are* "in over our heads." Only when we are pushed out beyond what *we* know, or what *we* can do, will we ever be forced to see that we are incomplete and inadequate without Christ.

Let me give you another picture to "hang on to". Let's say you are standing in the vicinity of a cliff, holding a rope labeled "The Good News." This rope claims to have the ability to hold you and keep you from falling. You are studying the rope as you stand about 100 yards away from the edge of the cliff. At that distance, does it really make any difference to you whether that rope will hold you or not? Not really. You don't have any plans to use it, and the ground is currently doing quite nicely at holding you up.

Now move over to the edge of the cliff. You have tied the rope securely to a rock and are contemplating climbing down the mountain. What are your thoughts now concerning the rope? I would wager you are a tad more anxious and *hopeful* about its claims. You hope it's going to hold you up. Are you sure? Not yet. What will it take to make you *sure* the rope will hold you? What would convince you that the rope is all the rope claims to be? You have to start climbing down the mountain and put your weight on it. Only then will you ever *know*.

Jesus is asking, "Do you want to *know* what it means to love others unconditionally? Then go where I'm sending you; to the one you just happen to hate the most and you will *have to* be filled with something beyond yourself in order to love that person. Set sail!"

"Do you want to be bold in your proclamation of the Good News? Then, for God and by His leading, find someone to tell your Good News. You will be surprised to discover that your stammering tongue has been equipped with power from on high. Set sail!"

"Do you want to experience a life submerged in the Spirit of God? Then go where I send you, out into the deep, go where and to what you can not handle on your own and you won't have any choice but to fling your arms wide open and invite Me in."

Last Spring, I went out to mow my lawn and discovered the riding lawn mower was broken. Since the grass was touching the lower ledge of the windows, I decided I had better mow it even if I had to use a push mower. Needless to say, our push mower does not see much action. It waits patiently until the rider breaks and I can't find another rider to borrow, and I turn to it as a last resort. I walked over to crank it up and low and behold it was out of gas. Why? Simple: No one puts gas into a machine that is not being used. It's only when we wipe off the cob webs and push the machine to the starting blocks that we bother to fill it with the power it needs to accomplish the work it has to do.

I guess the best, and my most recent example of being equipped *as* I set sail has been the writing of this book. I have already shared how the realization of this truth has been forming and growing in my heart over the years. Little by little, I have discovered what it means to be immersed in His Spirit. But never, and I do mean "never" have I been forced to stay in constant, non-interrupted communion with the Holy Spirit more than in the process of writing this book. I am not a writer. I am a speaker. I am not an intellectual theologian (as I'm sure you have surmised by now). I am one who simply tells what I have experienced, and sometimes not very clearly. I can't even spell for goodness sake. Thank heaven for spell checks and computers. But, -to paraphrase someone- "Where the Spirit of God called me, the Grace of God sustained me." It was out in the deep water, where Jesus told me to cast my nets,that I began to know *and experience* anew what it means to be immersed in Him.

"Set sail! The Captain's calling. It's time to climb on board. Set Sail."

CHAPTER 23

Keep Looking Ahead

"When they had finished eating, Jesus said to Simon Peter, 'Simon son of John, do you truly love me more than these?' 'Yes, Lord,' he said, 'you know that I love you.' Jesus said, 'Feed my lambs.' Again Jesus said, 'Simon son of John, do you truly love me?' He answered, 'Yes, Lord, you know that I love you.' Jesus said, 'Take care of my sheep.' The third time he said to him, 'Simon son of John, do you love me?' Peter was hurt because Jesus asked him the third time, 'Do you love me?' He said, 'Lord, you know all things; you know that I love you.' Jesus said, 'Feed my sheep.'"
(John 21:15-17 NIV)

For years, the biggest road block to my truly making some headway in getting out of the picture was my unwillingness to admit and deal with the fact that I had not gotten out of the picture *already*. In other words, because of stupid pride, when God would touch my heart with a sense of conviction that I had again gone my own way, and that there was much more growth that needed to take place in my relationship with Him, there was a little voice which said, "Wait a minute! You already made this commitment. You shouldn't have to do it again."

Actually, it's John Wesley's fault. John Wesley was to become the instigator of what would be one of the greatest Holy Spirit revivals in the world. At the start, however, Wesley was an intellectual snob who became a minister and missionary only because his mama wanted him to, and he thought he might be able to save his own soul in the process. Needless to say, his early ministry and mission work was a disaster. He was doing the reading and following the current methodologies of his day and the results were failure at every turn. He had never had a life changing experience which put him in relationship and communion with the God who was waiting to guide and empower his ministry.

Finally, he experienced new life in God, and from that point on, God literally shook the world through him. One minute he was a waste of skin and gave every minister a bad name. The next minute he was turning the world upside down for the Kingdom of God. My belief was that if it was instantaneous for him, and the results were obvious and *permanent*, then it should be the same for everyone else. **Wrong!**

I was wrong on two counts: First of all, I was wrong about how it would happen for me. As I said, the change was anything but instantaneous and permanent. Secondly, I was wrong in my perception of Wesley. Though general history -especially Methodist history- paints Wesley as a flawless saint after his full surrender to God, his own journals and the writing of his friends give the full picture. Basically, Wesley struggled just like everyone else. He had his days and weeks where he was a wide open vessel, ready to be used by the King. Then the tables would turn and he would slip back into a narrow-mindedness which threatened to kill the mighty movement of God which had been created through him.

It isn't instantaneous or permanent for *anyone*! Look at Wesley! Look at Paul! Paul said, "I press on". Look at Peter! One minute Peter was promising that though everyone else may desert Jesus in his hour of need, Peter never would. The next thing you know, Peter is running away from an inquisitive slave girl with roosters crowing in his ears. Everyone has their ups and downs as they grow in their relationship with God.

That is all well and good. But what's the difference between what is in this chapter and the point made in the opening chapter of this section about "getting out of the picture" being a **process**? Basically this: It's one thing to know that this filling -immersion- is a process, but it adds to the power of that knowledge to *acknowledge* that we have not *finished* that process. In other words, for some of us, one of the things we are going to have to do is face the fact that we are not as far along the path of immersion as we would like to think.

In a number of ways, this chapter is really intended for those who have been around awhile. What I mean by that is, when I was in my late teens and early twenties, though I did not like to hear that I had many things to learn and a long way to go in regards to *anything*, I was still semi-open to the fact that there were a number of things I needed to learn. As I moved into my later twenties and had been claiming for years to have experienced a complete infilling of God's Spirit -only to be proved wrong by my own witness- it was humbling and humiliating to realize that though *I had* moved a few steps forward in my walk, I was no where near the end. It wasn't until I could acknowledge and accept the fact that I had been fooling myself and playing religious games that I could finally do something about it.

I am discovering that this problem becomes more and more pronounced the older someone gets. The younger portions of my congregations are always much more ready to admit that they have wasted their lives and thrown away their years chasing after false philosophies or empty truths. It is easier for them to admit it because they have only a few years to regret. But slap on an extra 30 or 50 years of wallowing around in the shallows of Christianity, and it will take the crucifixion of one's pride to admit that there could have been, and should have been, more in one's life and relationship with God.

In essence, the point is this: Don't be like the king in the children's story who was unwilling to admit that he had been scammed and so pretended to see the invisible clothes. Everyone else could see he was naked. By the same token, everyone else can see we are naked as well. We must be willing to admit that in a variety of ways we have wasted some time -possibly years- and we still have a long way to go on the journey.

Hey! If you've denied Christ, admit it, ask forgiveness, and move on. Only when you do, can you hear and receive the words, "Feed My Sheep."

CHAPTER 24

The Gift or the Giver

"I am the vine; you are the branches. If a man remains in me and I in him, he will bear much fruit; apart from me you can do nothing. If anyone does not remain in me, he is like a branch that is thrown away and withers;..."
(John 15:5,6a NIV)

Hello! Welcome to a new part of this book. No longer are you reading the book "Immersed." You have now been teleported to the church, "Prepare to receive the Light, Faith Holiness, Church of the Virgin Birth, Pentecostal Personhood!" We are truly glad to have you along.

Do you need a new car? Is your house in disrepair? Do your kids have crooked teeth? Do you need a new job with a bigger salary and a company car? Does your dog have fleas? Most importantly, have you recently discovered that you have ring around the collar? WELL! my friend... and you know you are my friends; all of these problems, and more, can be taken care of here at "Prepare to receive the Light, Faith Holiness, Church of the Virgin Birth, Pentecostal Personhood!" All you have to do is *believe* and you will *receive*!!

Sounds a little sacrilegious doesn't it. Whoever heard of one's faith clearing up a flea problem or getting rid of ring around the collar? Substitute another church name, however, a few different problems, and you can hear that type of pitch regularly on television and radio. Don't believe me? You haven't been paying attention. Not too long ago I heard a minister running across a stage, ranting and raving, saying, "I have a $500 suit, a $600 Rolex watch, a brand new Mercedes, and you can too! I have all of this because of Jesus!"

The crowd sent up a whooping "Amen", and "Hallelujah!" Then he said, "You can have prosperity! You can have that new car! You can have that bulging bank account, and unbelievable personal happiness with everything your heart desires! Why? Because God loves you and wants you to have it! How? Just believe in Jesus! Ask Him ..... and send my ministry money, and you will *receive*!"

The crowd was going wild. They were eating it up!

They were eating it up basically because it was what they wanted to hear. If you think about it, who wouldn't want to be told that all we needed to do was meet a few requirements, believe a few beliefs, and all of our desires would be met?

All I can say is that type of preaching and belief is garbage! Nowhere does it say in God's Word that we will get everything our little, spoiled hearts desire if we simply rub God's tummy just right and say all the proper words. What is going on is exactly what Paul warned about when he said that people will gather those around them who tell them what their itching ears want to hear. At best, this "Gospel of Prosperity" is a misunderstanding of Jesus' promise. At worst, it is a sham and a scam perpetrated by manipulators to suck in a big, gullible audience and bleed them dry.

How all of that fits into this section is very simple: There is a market for this manipulative bunk due to the fact that many of us tend to focus our attention and desires on the *gifts* and not the *Giver*. In other words, when we think of why we should become a Christian, we often think of what we are going to get out of it -the gifts- instead of simply being in relationship with the Giver -God.

Think of a Christian witness or testimony you might have heard recently. Most often the person sharing their testimony will talk about the wonderful peace they have come to find, or the joy they now realize. Sometimes Christians will talk about a miraculous healing or a moving inspiration he or she has received. When I was in college, someone once stood and gave God praise for the $100 he had just received in the mail in answer to his desperate need for money. In most testimonies, the focus is *what* God has blessed the receiver with.

Take a look at a few of the chapters in the beginning of this book. They are filled with the "gifts" or residual effects of being immersed in the Spirit of God. There is, of course, nothing wrong with emphasizing and giving God praise for the gifts. There is not a doubt in my mind that during my college years, God *did* have a direct hand in those young people receiving the money for which they gave God praise. The problem, and the road block to our getting out of the picture, comes when our desire is not necessarily to be in a growing relationship with The Master, but rather for that which the Master can give.

A good illustration of this was my Dad. My dad was a pretty talented person. He could fix broken bikes, chase off bullies, give advice about girls, play a little ball, and, of course, earn the money to buy the Christmas presents. The one negative thing I remember from my early childhood was that my father traveled a great deal in his job as evangelist for the General Board of Discipleship. He traveled primarily around the United States. However, every once in awhile he had the opportunity to venture overseas. It really did not matter where my father went or what he did when he was there. We -my brother and I- really did not care. What was important was what he brought us when he came home.

The story was always the same. After he had been gone for most of the week, doing a revival in Timbuktu, my brother and I would start getting excited and anxious for him to get in from the airport. My dad would walk in the door, yell, "I'm home!" and we would come tearing through the house. There was no, "Dad we're glad to see you!" or "Hurray! You're home!" We ran up to him with greed in our eyes and sweat on our palms. We wanted to know what he had brought us.

In his good-natured way he would almost always say, "What? No hug for your dad?" My brother and I would both get one of those smirky looks on our faces which said, "Well, if we have to," and then barely touch my father in a half-hearted hug. Having done our duty, we would then quickly grab the goods and run off, leaving my father standing in the doorway, alone.

Our focus was not the giver, but the gifts. My dad's value -at that time- was not based on who he was, but on what he could give us.

There are two things about that story I want to make sure you get. First of all, it is probably needless to point out how that made my father feel. "Unappreciated" and "taken for granted" just barely begin to scratch the surface of how he felt standing there alone in the doorway.

Secondly, now that he is no longer around, -he died in 1988- I would give anything to have in my personal memory banks, not a recollection of what toy or souvenir he gave me, but rather a memory of my climbing up in his lap, and spending time with a father I had missed.... and miss.

If we want to truly grow closer to God, be immersed in God's Spirit, and get out of the picture, we need to want *God*, and not what God can do for us.

Let's put it in practical terms. Say that you are currently single. You have been out of college for a few years and have dated around, but still have not found the right person. One day, you are set up on a blind date. The only reason you even entertained the idea of going on this date was because of your friend's build up of the person you were to meet. Your friend described this person as giving, compassionate, caring, smart, witty, a good money earner, and blessed with above average oral hygiene. You are not only interested in this person because of what blessings this person could be to your daily life, but the more you hear, the more you realize that this person would be a perfect mate considering your professional plans. You finally meet this wonder person and she -or he- is all your friend said, and more. You have the natural reaction of getting all goose-pimply, woosied-legged, and tongue-tied. It's love, and you know it. After a few months, you propose marriage. This wonderful person says "Yes". You honeymoon, set up house, and get down to the business of being married.

Let me ask you this question: What type of marriage will it be if your only feelings towards your spouse are based on what she or he could do for you? You would *still* be married! At times you would even be happy, especially when this wonderful person was doing things for you. But the question is: Are you united? Are you really in a relationship? Are you truly experiencing everything there is to experience in a marriage? The answer is "NO!"

What makes a marriage a *real* marriage; what gives true blessing and joy to everyone involved in the marriage is if the foundation of your relationship is based on the desire to *be* with that other person regardless of what he or she can produce for you. Anything less than that is only scratching the surface of what *could be* in a marriage.

The same is true for faith. As long as our desire to be in a relationship with God is based on what God can give *to* us or do *for* us, we will never know what it truly means to be *in* relationship and immersed in the Spirit of God.

A good biblical example of what I am talking about is the story of the fiery furnace in the third chapter of Daniel. According to the story, because of the young Hebrew men's faithfulness to God, God had moved them into prominent positions in the government of Nebuchadnezzar. Those who had been in those positions became jealous that a group of exiles should move to so high a power in their homeland.

One day, Nebuchadnezzar decided that he wanted to go on an ego trip. He had a huge statue of himself erected and ordered that at the appropriate signal, everyone in the land was to bow and pay homage to the statue. Everyone obeyed except the three Hebrew exiles. It does not take a rocket scientist to figure out what happened next. Because of their jealousy, the once prominent leaders "tattled" on the Hebrews and told Nebuchadnezzar that these disobedient foreigners were not bowing before the statue.

Nebuchadnezzar became furious, called the men into his presence, gave them another chance, and in so doing said, "If you do not worship it, you will be thrown immediately into a blazing furnace. Then what god will be able to rescue you from my hand?" (Daniel 3:15b NIV) Their response is the key point here. They responded:

> "O Nebuchadnezzar, we do not need to defend ourselves before
> you in this matter. If we are thrown into the blazing furnace,
> the God we serve is able to save us from it, and he will rescue
> us from your hand, O king." (Daniel 3:16b,17 NIV)

That sounds pretty good. If you read it carefully, it sounds a little like what the Gospel of Prosperity preachers preach: God is powerful enough to do and give us anything. "But wait a minute!" you might say. "What about the Hebrew men's response? They obviously are basing their faith on what God can do!"

Good point. The sad thing is that when I hear points made from this scripture, most often the "point maker" stops where I stopped. Here is the rest of their response to the king:

> "BUT even if he does not, we want you to know, O king,
> that we will not serve your gods or worship the image of gold
> you have set up."

WOW! Go back and read that again. Did you catch it?! They did not say, "He will rescue us from your hand, O king, and so we claim it with all the right words and thus make it so."

Neither did they say, "..... O king, he will do this because we deserve it since we have blessed God with our presence and devotion." They said, "But even if he does NOT!..."

WOW! How can they say that? Are they so shallow in faith that they are making an out for themselves in order to explain it away if God does not perform? Probably not. Probably not, if for no other reason than they would not have much time to be embarrassed since they were to be "immediately" thrown into a fiery furnace.

Were they simply demonstrating their own personal defiance of the king? Could be. But unlikely.

How could they say such a thing? Simple: Their relationship and consequent devotion to God was not based on whether God could get them out of a jam or not. They were going to remain faithful to God because God was God. Being immersed in His Spirit was what gave them life. Everything else was just icing on the cake.

How? How do we begin the process of getting out of the picture and being immersed in the Spirit of God? Make sure it is the Spirit of God we seek.

CHAPTER 25

You can't fly with eagles if you hang around with turkeys

"Listen! A farmer went out to sow his seed. As he was scattering the seed, some fell along the path, and the birds came and ate it up. Some fell on rocky places, where it did not have much soil. It sprang up quickly, because the soil was shallow. But when the sun came up, the plants were scorched, and they withered because they had no root. Other seed fell among thorns, which grew up and choked the plants, so that they did not bear grain." (Mark 4:3-7 NIV)

My father used to say, "If you want to be a basketball player, then you are going to have to hang out with basketball players. If you want to be a scientist, then you need to hang out with scientists. If you want to be an idiot, then you have to hang out with idiots. And, if you want to be a Christian, then you are going to have to hang out with Christians."

His point was that we tend to take on the personalities, priorities, and make-up of what we expose ourselves to. The scary thing is that he was absolutely right. Psychological studies have been supporting this idea for years. Common sense is also standing in the corner of the belief that we will become what we expose ourselves to. It is true. If you want to become a filthy-mouthed jerk, then...... Well, you get the point.

A few years ago, a friend of mine gave me a book by Peter Lord entitled *Turkeys and Eagles*. Basically, the book was about two eaglets who were accidentally thrown into a herd of turkeys. Because they were so young, and because turkeyism was all that they knew, these little eaglets took it upon themselves to become the best turkeys they could. Though their instincts told them to soar, they did their best to learn the waddle of their apparent peers. Though everything in them was urging them to hunt and stalk, they tried to make themselves content with pecking at the ground and periodically stepping out in the fast lane and foraging for berries. In every respect, they worked towards becoming the best turkeys they could be. Actually, they made pretty good turkeys once they got the hang of it.

Is it possible? Could eagles really be trained to act like turkeys? Certainly! There has been account after account of animals who "bond" with another species and try to model the traits they observe. For example, there was the duck who bonded with a dog, and instead of quacking and swimming, he barked and dug in the dirt. There was my Aunt's dog who bonded with my aunt and thought it was human. There was the young boy who bonded with a group of thugs and wound up non-human. The evidence is overwhelming: We tend to become what we expose ourselves to.

Let's take a look at one of my all time favorite Biblical examples: Solomon. For those of you who are not in the know, Solomon was the third king of Israel. After the throne was removed from the family of Saul, it was given to David with the promise that as long as his family remained faithful to God, there would always be a descendent of David on the throne. As the account goes, David had a wandering eye, and it wandered in the direction of Bethsheba who was an exhibitionist. She liked to take baths outside where the neighbors could see her. David "got together" with Bethsheba, and after losing one child, finally gave birth to the bouncing baby Solomon. By some strange twists of fate, as well as God's unexplainable will, Solomon took the throne after David's death.

At first, everything looked hunky-dory for Solomon. He, like David, for the most part, was a man after God's own heart. When God asked Solomon what he wanted most, instead of asking for riches or fame, Solomon asked God for the wisdom to rule God's people well. God was thrilled with

Solomon's request, and not only gave him the wisdom he requested, but the riches and fame as well. According to the account in I Kings, people came from near and far to sit in Solomon's presence and be blessed by his wisdom and insights.

So far so good. The country was extending its borders, the people were at peace, the temple was built, a new palace was erected, and God was blessing everything Solomon did. Here is the account according to I Kings 10:14: "The weight of gold that Solomon received yearly was 666 talents, not including the revenues from merchants and traders from all the Arabian kings and the governors of the land.... (verse 23) Solomon was greater in riches and wisdom than all the other kings of the earth."

What happened? How does the splendor of Solomon fit into the point of this chapter? Easy: Solomon, like his father, liked the ladies. Not only did he like the ladies, but he understood the political wisdom of solidifying unions between governments through royal marriages. Solomon was more than willing to "sacrifice himself" for the sake of his country by marrying the daughters of the surrounding kings. Once he had a few wives, he figured one or two hundred more would not make that much of a difference. It started off slowly, but by the time Solomon was done, according to I Kings 11:3, he had seven hundred wives of royal birth and three hundred concubines. That is quite a harem by any standard.

So, Solomon liked the ladies. It was an accepted practice to have more than one wife. Though the Isrealites could have more than one wife, they were strictly forbidden to intermarry with the surrounding people. The sole reason for this restriction was to keep the faith pure. The command -listed over and over in the first five books of the Bible- usually went something like this: "You shall not intermarry with the nations around you because they will lead your hearts astray." It should not be surprising that I Kings 11:3 reads in its entirety: "He had seven hundred wives of royal birth and three hundred concubines, **and his wives led him astray.**"

If you want to be a basketball player, hang around with basketball players. If you want to be an idiot, hang around with idiots. If you want to be a turkey, hang around with turkeys. If you want to be led astray from the Lord, hang around with 700 wives of royal birth who worship other gods. The point is we *do* tend to become what we expose ourselves to.

Hopefully, it is apparent what this has to do with, "How do we continue the process of getting out of the picture?" Don't hang around with turkeys or the things of turkeys. This is a part of the message of the parable of the sower. Shallow soil begets shallow believers who get "burned out" easily. Seed sown and allowed to grow along with the weeds, will beget a plant which will eventually be choked out. If we want the plant to grow, and more importantly, to produce, it needs to be in soil free of forces which will choke out its life.

Though it is not the deepest illustration there is, one negative illustration of this point is R-rated movies. Before becoming a Christian, I had a mouth like a sewer. As the old saying goes, "I could cuss wallpaper off the wall." It was really rather pathetic. Except in the presence of adult figures, I would guess that every eighth word was profane. Personally, I agree with the person who said, "Profanity is the attempt of a feeble mind to express itself forcefully." Simply put, I was too addlebrained to think of any other way to express myself.

Whatever the cause, I did have a filthy mouth. When I gave my life to Christ, that was one of the first things to go. In fact, of all the things I heard from others about the difference in my life, more people made remarks about the lack of dirty language in my vocabulary than anything else. It seemed that the Spirit helped clean up that room first and foremost. However, to this very day, I cannot watch R or PG-13 rated movies because of the profanity. The reason is not that I start talking that garbage all over again. Although I am a little worried now and then that something might slip in an

Administrative Board or Pastor Parish Relations meeting, the reason I cannot watch movies with profanity is because the words start running around in my mind and I find myself thinking them. It is hard to stay closely connected to God when foul words are running through your thoughts.

My solution? Stop hanging around with turkeys!

Is your problem gossip? Then you might have to either confront or stop that "prayer group" that feels it necessary to share every little sordid detail when making a prayer request.

Is your problem greed? Then the group at the club might have to go from your social schedule for awhile. You can't fly with eagles if you hang around with turkeys.

Am I saying then that we need to separate ourselves from the world altogether? Hardly! Paul basically says in his letters that we can not remove ourselves completely from the world in which we live. In fact, Paul taught that we needed to stay in contact with the world in order to reach the world for Jesus. Paul knew, as would anyone with common sense, that the world will never be reached for Jesus if Christians stay locked up in their safe cocoons, afraid of interaction for fear of contamination. However, while it is necessary that Christians continue to be a part of the world, it is destructive to our faith to allow the world to again become a part of us.

How can we do that? With so much "turkey stuff" bombarding us regularly, how do we continue to be faithful in reaching the "turkeys" without becoming one again?

HANG AROUND WITH EAGLES! Remember? If you want to be an idiot, then hang around with idiots. If you want to be a Christian, then hang around with Christians.

One of the most heart wrenching aspects of ministry is taking people off on spiritual retreats and ministry events, only to return them to the same humdrum atmosphere they left. It is always the same. Every time a group returns and God has moved us and used us in wonderful ways, someone -if not everyone- will say, "It's so hard to come back to where everyone is so dead. Why can't it be like it was this past week all the time?"

My usual response to these questions/remarks is, "It can be!"

"Home" *can be* or can have the same spiritually rejuvenating environment most people find on retreats and special ministries. Home can be *if* we make more of a concerted effort to expose ourselves to the soil which will create that environment in us.

Why go to church? Because your spouse nags you to death, or you can get your mom off your back? Should we go to church in order to help bolster the attendance numbers and help make the preacher look good. Well, there is some justification in that.

Just a little joke there.

We need to go to a regular gathering of Christians so we can have opportunity after opportunity to hang around with eagles.

Read the Word. Pick up one of the millions of excellent Christian books now available. Talk about Jesus in casual conversation. Listen to Christian music -contemporary and otherwise. Attend a Bible study. Pray. Pray individually and with others.

How do we start and continue the process of getting out of the picture? Put yourself in the proper soil which will foster growth.

Hang around with eagles and with the things of eagles.

CHAPTER 26
Scraping the Pot

"For whoever wants to save his life will lose it, but whoever loses his life for me will find it." (Matthew 16:25 NIV)

If the goal of our faith is making room in our "picture" for God to pour His Spirit fully into our hearts and souls, then we have to undergo the process of getting rid of the "gunk" that now resides in our picture. The problem is that we kind of like our gunk right where it is.

We like our gunky *gossipiness* because it insures that we have more information than others, and information is power.

We like our slimy *pettiness* because it helps us get our way most of the time. Most people are either too squeamish or to mature to lower themselves into a petty argument, so they give in. What does it matter what people think of us as long as we get what we want?

We like our pathetic *prejudice* because it keeps the "undesirables" at arm's length.

We like our *mean-spiritedness* because it keeps the people around us on their toes and gives us a sense of authority and control. There are very few things as pleasing as having an entire room tense up when we walk in or having people jump when we speak. So what if they don't like us. They respect us, supposedly.

We like our *shallow commitment* right where it is. How many people really like to be around a "Jesus freak"? We fit in better when we blend in.

You get the point.   In many respects we are comfortable with the trash that is in us. It may not be pretty trash, but it has two things going for it: 1) It is familiar. 2) It gives us a sense of control. Yet, Jesus says that in order to find our lives, we have to lose our lives.

There is one problem with the typical translation of "lose your life". It is not accurate. "Lose" is such a weak translation of the original word used. The definition of the Greek word Jesus uses *can* mean "lose," but the essence of the word means "to kill" or "to utterly destroy." "Lose" is at the same level of meaning for the Greek word used as "appreciate" is for "love." Love can mean to appreciate, but its deeper meaning is to feel for another person to the point you would give of yourself for their benefit. With this new definition of "lose", read the scripture again: "For whoever wants to save his life -pluck it out of destruction- will kill it, or utterly destroy it, but whoever kills his life for me will find it." Jesus is saying that if we want the picture filled with the presence and Spirit of God, then we need to destroy the gunk that is presently taking up room.

However, since we *are* so comfortable with the gunk inside our picture, the process of destroying it is often rather uncomfortable. In order to move forward in the "getting out of the picture" process, we have to be willing to deal with the "uncomfortableness."

Ah! Let's be frank! Most of the time, getting the gunk out just down right hurts! When glass is repaired, it must be melted. When metal is welded together, it has to be heated. When a muscle is strengthened, it must always meet resistance. When gold is refined, it goes through the fire in order to burn off the dross. When the ungodly gunk in Christians' lives is destroyed and we are made holy, often it is through, and because of, trials.

Peter wrote:

"In this you greatly rejoice, though now for a little while you may have had to suffer grief in all kinds of trials. These have come so that your faith -of greater worth than gold, which perishes even though refined by fire- may be proved genuine and may result in praise, glory and honor when Jesus Christ is revealed." (I Peter 1:6,7 NIV)

Think of a pot used to take scrap food out to a dog.

First of all, let me point out that this illustration is completely hypothetical. This has never happened in my house. It is only a story I heard from a friend of mine. The names have been changed to protect the innocent.

Let's say you have a pot in which you are collecting scraps of food for your dog. The pot was originally used to cook mashed potatoes. After supper, the scraps were collected, put in the pot and then a certain person in the household was asked to take it immediately to the dog. Let's say that certain person neglected his -OR HER- duty, and left the pot on the counter for, oh.... three days. During that period, the other significant other in the family was unwilling to do the chore this certain person promised to do. The scraps continued to accumulate in the pot. By the time this certain person decides to walk the fifty feet to the dog's lot and give the scraps to the dog, it has been three days, and the scraps -particularly the mashed potatoes- have solidified and have moved in the direction of petrification.

Please note that the dog was fed in that three day period. The dog was just not fed the scraps. I want to point this out so that my friend does not have the animal control people come down on him.

Are you getting the picture? For those of you who are scrap pot couriers, what happened when our hero reached the dog lot and turned the pot upside down? Simple: The gooey, mushy insides came out easily with a "plop." But, the hard, crusty, unidentifiable material that remained was left clinging to the sides like bubble gum to braces.

How did our hero get the hard, crusty material off the sides? He scrapped it! He scraped it *real* hard! He had to. Otherwise the pot would never have been usable for anything else. In order to make room for what it was intended for, the gunk that was clinging to the sides had to be removed. Even if that meant using a knife, scouring it with a Brillo pad, and then washing it in boiling water. If the pot would have said, "No! I don't want to be scraped," that pot would probably still be sitting on a shelf somewhere wondering why it is never used. You can't fill something up that is already filled with something else.

"For whoever would *utterly scrape the gunk out of* (italics my paraphrase) his life for me will find it!"

This is really the essence of the rich young ruler story. You remember the account. A rich man comes to Jesus and asks how he might find eternal life. Jesus tells him to follow the commands. "No problem," he basically responds. "All of these I have kept," the young man said. "What do I still lack?" (Matthew 19:20 NIV)

What the young man had done up to that point was walk to the dog lot with his pot of scraps and dump out the gooey, mushy, *easy to remove* portions. He had the time. He had the money. He had the right support. He could keep these silly little laws. "No problem. I can get rid of this gooey gunk easily. There's still a burden on my soul, however, that I'm not finished yet."

Jesus knew what the problem was. He had gotten rid of the easy gunk, yes. What still remained was the caked on, crusty stuff that had merged itself deeply into his life. Jesus looked right into his soul, saw the problem and said, "If you want to be *perfect*, go, sell your possessions, and give to the poor, and you will have treasure in heaven. Then come, follow me." (Matthew 19:21 NIV)

Was Jesus saying that giving money and possessions away will bring us into a perfect relationship with God? NOPE! Sorry! Believe it or not, that is too easy. But it was not easy for the rich young ruler. His money, and the security and self-value he found in it were his particular problems. In order to have room for the Spirit to be poured into him and, as Jesus said, to become *perfect*, the man's particular, crusty gunk -his love of money- was going to have to be painfully scraped away from his soul.

What happened? The same thing that could happen to any of us. The rich young ruler was unwilling to pay the price, to undergo the pain, and so he just walked away.

It is often through the fire, at times experiencing great pain, that the dross is burned away and what remains is holy. However, knowing this is only a small portion of the battle. Being willing to see it through is the rough part.

As I was writing the chapter on finding our value in God alone, I was constantly reminded of the fiery process I went through to discover that wonderfully liberating truth. As I have said, for years I pictured myself eventually becoming a "successful" minister. I envisioned hundreds and possibly thousands moved because of my great sermons and marvelous insights. Though God did use my stumbling, bumbling ministry despite my immature and insecure arrogance, things were not progressing on the time table that I had set for myself. In fact, they ground to a screeching halt when I reached a particular appointment.

At this appointment, it was communicated to me, in no uncertain terms, that my ministry, my personality, and what little Godly vision I had was an unwelcome commodity in that community. Though there were some who were supportive, they were in the silent minority and were content, for the most part, to stay there. After only a few months or so, the only thing that was getting me through was the constant thought that I could quit the ministry and do something else. Anything else would have been fine at that point.

It was a long process. The fire was hot. The months and years, in many ways, were painful and heart wrenching. But, hallelujah, in the midst of the fire, I began -emphasizing the word "began"- to see a nugget being exposed. The nugget was the essence of the chapter on finding my value in God. With that nugget I found new power, enthusiasm, and perseverance.

Though I would not have a desire to go through that fire again, I would reluctantly be willing to go through it because I now know that on the other side the Master Metal Worker is preparing a holy vessel for The King.

Are you willing to undergo the fire? If not, pray for strength.

This may sound even more strange: Are you willing to pray that the fire would come?

Remember, if our final goal is total immersion in the Spirit of God, and if a part of that being immersed takes place only when we undergo the fire, *why not* pray that the fire would come? We can only imagine what the Master Metal Worker has in mind when we are taken out and cooled. Keep in mind what C.S. Lewis once said, "God whispers in our pleasures, speaks in our conscience and shouts in our pain. It is the megaphone to arouse a deaf world."

CHAPTER 27
Break

"Now Naaman was commander of the army of the king of Aram. He was a great man in the sight of his master and highly regarded, because through him the Lord had given victory to Aram. He was a valiant soldier, but he had leprosy." (II Kings 5:1 NIV)

The story of Naaman from the Old Testament has always been a favorite of mine. The story is fairly simple. Naaman was a valiant and brave commander of the army of the king of Aram. He probably was handsome, strong, and good at Tidily Winks. Naaman had one problem. He had leprosy. This was not some small inconvenience. Because the disease was believed to be contagious, people who had leprosy were banished from society. All of what Naaman was and what he hoped to be hinged on getting cured of this deadly disease.

On the advice of the King's wise men and advisors, Naaman tried every known home remedy in his kingdom, and probably a few unknown ones as well. Nothing worked. Somewhere along the way he heard about a prophet in Israel named Elisha. He heard that this prophet was a great and powerful man, and that many miracles and healings had been attributed to him. Someone suggested that Namaan go down to Israel and see what Elisha would say.

It is important to realize that going down to Israel was quite a sacrifice for Naaman. It was not every day a leading power in a conquering kingdom would lower himself to talk to a wandering nomad in a subject nation. But since Naaman was getting desperate, he went, whether he liked it or not.

You can almost see Namaan riding up to Elisha's tent with his entourage of attendants and servants. Since Naaman was a powerful figure of authority, he surely expected Elisha to come out when he was at a respectful distance and greet him before he dismounted. When Naaman arrived in the camp, however, Elisha was nowhere to be seen. A little disgusted, Naaman dismounts and walks up to Elisha's tent. Maybe Elisha was sleeping and did not realize who was "blessing him" with his presence. Naaman yells to Elisha that he, the great leader of the armies of Aram, had arrived and wished to talk with him. Naaman's announcement is met with nothing but silence. Naaman hears a little rustling in the tent. Elisha is taking too long, so Naaman bellows again for Elisha to come and greet him. The flap lifts and out walks Elisha's...*servant*!

Of all the nerve! Apparently, Elisha was too busy with other matters to be bothered with a simple healing of leprosy. So, he sent his servant out to tell Naaman what he should do. Of course, this blatant lack of respect infuriated Naaman. How dare Elisha not appear himself to perform the healing. Naaman was getting desperate though, so at least he listened to what the servant had to say. The message was simple: "Go wash yourself seven times in the Jordan, and your flesh will be restored, and you will be cleansed."

You can almost hear Naaman say, "That's it!? I come all this way and your boss not only doesn't come out to meet me, but tells me to go and wash in some stinky, dirty river? I can't believe this!"

Not only was Naaman a bit disturbed about the instructions to wash in the dirty Jordan River, but he was equally disappointed that Elisha did not come out and do some magical little voodoo in order to cure the leprosy in a spectacular fashion. Here is what Naaman said according to II Kings 5:11 & 12, "I thought that he would surely come out to me and stand and call on the name of the Lord his God, wave his hand over the spot and cure me of my leprosy. Are not Abana and Pharpar, the rivers of Damascus, better than any of the waters of Israel? Couldn't I wash in them and be cleansed?" After saying this very intelligent statement, II Kings says he turned and walked away "in a rage". He was desperate, but not *that* desperate.

Ah, but wait! Wisdom prevails! One of Naaman's servants came and tactfully said, "Naaman, you big, stupid ox, if the prophet would have come out and asked you to do something extravagant and flashy, you would have gone along with it. As it is, he has asked you to do something very simple. I know you have a simple mind and linear thought is difficult for you, but don't you think you ought to at least give it a try?" (I hope you know portions of the above quote were added by dramatic license. You do get the gist of what the servant said, however.)

Naaman strained his brain, and finally admitted that he should at least give it a try. He was dirty. He was shamed. He was dying, and anything would be better than his current situation. He went. He washed, and he was cleansed.... just like the prophet said he would be.

So, what's the point of this story for this chapter? What does a pride-filled Aramaic military leader with leprosy have to do with our getting out of the picture and being immersed in the Spirit of God? The reason Naaman finally gave in, and despite all of his tradition, pride, and prejudice, followed Elisha's instructions, was that Naaman was **desperate**.

Yes, I said *desperate*. Any other day, if Naaman's' life and livelihood had not been threatened by this disease, he would have run the prophet through with his sword and called it a successful racial cleansing. Being sick made him look for help. His inability to cure himself forced him look for help anywhere. The fact that he had nowhere else to turn ultimately led to his following Elisha's instructions and bathing in the dirty Jordan River. He was desperate.

How does that apply to us? It applies in this way: In order to fully surrender to God and let the picture totally reflect Him, we must reach a point where we are desperate enough to make that surrender.

We must be broken.

I know this sounds a little fanatical, but the record supports it. In the history of Israel, when were the people the most faithful? When did they make most of their promises to follow God and be obedient to His commands? Most of the time it was when they were flat on their backs, with the sword of some foreign kingdom at their throats, and they had no other place to look but up.

Someone might point out the times when the people were marching into the promised land and they took the time to set up a number of worship centers and recommit to the covenant. But even in those situations, the people were in desperate straits. First, they were greatly outnumbered. They were a wandering band of ex-slaves facing secured, well armed people behind brick walls. You bet they were going to keep in close contact with God. They knew they were in over their heads and needed all the help they could get. You could say they were.... Uh... desperate.

Moses recognized this tendency and our need. Take a few minutes to read the sixth chapter of Deuteronomy. Moses is telling the people that God needs to be first. He tells them that they are about to enter a land that was not theirs; occupy houses they did not build, and harvest fruits which they did not labor to produce. Then Moses says in verse 10, "When the Lord your God brings you into the land he swore to your fathers,.... then when you eat and are satisfied, be careful that you do not forget the Lord, who brought you out of Egypt, out of the land of slavery." Moses knew that when people become comfortable, safe, and satisfied, we tend to forget the Lord until another disaster strikes.

There are too many examples of this fact to cite them all, but I frequently see these examples played out over and over again in hospital rooms and funeral homes. It is amazing how "spiritual" people become when either they, or a loved one, is sick.

I remember my C.P.E. (Clinical Pastoral Education) work in Georgia Baptist Hospital in Atlanta, Georgia. In short, I was a chaplain in the hospital and was being trained to deal with all the horrors and triumphs of sickness. There was one gentlemen I will always remember. I was making my rounds on the floor I was assigned, and was just about to walk into this gentleman's room when the nurse down the hall whistled and waved me over to her station. She said, "Since you are new here, I figured I had better warn you. Mr. Simpson is not a very fun patient. He's cold, mean, angry, and takes it out on everyone." She paused. "I just thought you might like to know."

I may have needed to know, but I sure did not *want* to know that particular bit of information just before I walked into his room. I was desperately praying for the pager on my hip to go off and save me from certain death. No such luck. Where is a good miracle when you need it?

I walked into Mr. Simpson's room expecting a good cursing. I found Mr. Simpson sitting up in his bed, wearing a bathrobe, and staring out the window. I wondered why -if God were truly just- Mr. Simpson could not have been asleep. I tapped on the door and made my way into the room as Mr. Simpson turned to face me.

The eyes I looked into were not the eyes of a cold, mean, and angry man. What I saw was pain, fear, and desperation. I introduced myself, told him I was with the chaplain's office -something I am sure the chaplain's office denied a number of times on my behalf- and that I had just come by to see how he was doing. He swung around on his bed to face me, pulled the chair which was beside the bed up next to him so that I could sit down and said, "Please, have a seat. You are just the person I want to talk to."

To tell you the truth, my mind was doing a few "could this be" scenarios. I wondered if this could be a little test by the chaplains. I wondered if maybe I was on candid camera. I wondered if I was in the right room. What the nurses told me, and what I found in that room were on completely opposite poles. I tried to regain my concentration and at least appear to know what I was doing. To his remark about my being just the person he wanted to talk to, I responded with the very intelligent and inspiring, "Oh?"

For the next hour or so, I sat quietly and listened to this man tell me about his life. He talked about how he was taught to "look out for number one." He had used his selfish drive to work his way to the top, stepping on everyone and anyone who got in his way. He had been married twice. The reason he divorced was that he considered his wives not "good enough for him." He smiled a bit at the irony of that statement. He admitted that he really did not like people and wondered why there were so many who were such a drain on society. Our conversation continued to go on along these line for about an hour. After his long dissertation about how wonderful he was and his philosophy of life, he paused. He paused for a long time. He looked down at the bed and fiddled with the sheets. He glanced out the window and his eyes appeared to be staring at a distant billboard with some secret message. When he turned back to me, his eyes were wide and wet.

He did not cry. I'm not sure someone who had been that hard all of his life could still use his tear ducts. His eyes did not shed tears, but I could tell his spirit was shedding bucketfuls. He said, "Now, I'm sick. No! I'm not just sick. I'm dying. I'm dying of cancer and it's going to be long, hard, and painful. My money won't help. It will buy the best doctors, but even they can't stop the inevitable. My power doesn't make a bit of difference here. These people don't care what I did. To them I'm just another naked body to prod, draped in a hospital gown."

Another pause while he looked right into my soul.

"I'm dying," he said again. "Now I have to ask, What's the use? What do I do now?"

I sat there keeping eye contact with him as best as I could. He was waiting for me to give him some deep insight.

The only thing registering in my mind was, "MOMMY!! Get me out of this!! AHHHHH!"

I knew that would not help him much, so I just sat there.

Finally, he said, "Do I need to turn to God. I have never had much use for God. I never really believed there was a god. I may not believe completely now... but I sure do hope there is. Is God the answer?"

It was at that time my superb psychiatric and pastoral counseling training kicked in. I said what every qualified counselor would say at that point, "What do you think?"

He continued to look at me and said, "I think I need God. Now, tell me about Him."

I thought to myself, "I can handle this." Though I have not always been a big fan of volunteering my witness to people who have not asked, when someone requests it, I am the right guy. I briefly shared with him my faith story and my relationship with Jesus Christ. I talked about my struggles and doubt; about my triumphs and steps of faith. The more I talked, the more relaxed he seemed to become. When I finished, I stumbled through asking him if he wanted to know God now. Alas, like Naaman with Elijah, he was desperate, but not *that* desperate...yet.

He said, "Thanks. I wish I could. I'll have to think about it. Can you come back and see me?"

I assured him that I could. We had a prayer, and I went outside and threw up. Though I have gotten much better about this, to date, I would rather speak to 10,000 people than to share my faith one-on-one.

For the next week or so, I went by his room every day on my rounds. We talked about faith, life, and the Braves. I watched him very quickly take a turn for the worse. He was dying faster than the doctors thought he would. About three weeks after our first conversation, I returned to the hospital following a week long school break. When I was about to start my shift, I found a note for me in the Chaplain's office. I asked the secretary about it and she said that a man in the cancer ward had been calling down there for the last week or so wanting to talk with me. When other chaplains went to the room, he refused to talk. He wanted to talk only with me. Being the rookie in the bunch, I glanced over to my seasoned superiors and smiled.

Yes, pride is an ever-present thing.

I rushed upstairs, walked in his room, and found a bright, smiling man sitting where there was once a shriveled spirit. He said, "Where the.... Oh, excuse me. Where have you been?!"

"School break." I answered.

"I've been waiting to tell you the news! I gave my life to God! It was great! No one was here. No one said anything at the time. I just decided one night I wanted to give my life to Him, and I did!" he said.

I smiled and asked, "Well, how do you feel?"

"GREAT!" he almost shouted. "It's wonderful! I feel free, new...." his voice trailed off. Then he looked at me and asked, "Why did I wait so long?"

What came out of my mouth was not mine. The Lord said through me, "*You* weren't ready. But you didn't wait *too* long."

We talked, laughed, and argued a little about politics and the Braves. I left feeling euphoric. Mr. Simpson died the next week. He left no living relatives that I knew of. He left no children. But he left as a born-again child of God.

Why?

He *broke* just in time.

A gentleman in one of my churches said it best, "What we need is a good war, or another depression to wake people up." Though it sounds callous, that man is exactly right. If our goal is to be in relationship with God, what we need is to be broken. It is when we are broken that we tend to seek a relationship with God. Without brokeness or desperation we *most often* stay in the shallows and pat ourselves on the back at our "blessedness." As long as we feel "blessed" we most likely feel content and *self* sufficient. If we are self-sufficient, we will never see a need for God. If we never see a need for God, we will never *want* that relationship, much less have a desire to be immersed in His Spirit. In order for us to want *any*thing, we must first become disillusioned with the other options. This is especially true when it comes to a relationship with God.

As long as we still believe we can find comfort and security in how much we earn, we will never fully turn to God to find comfort and security.

As long as we still believe we can find fulfillment and peace in our job and in the amount of money we make, we will never turn to God to find fulfillment and peace.

As long as we still believe we can find value in our family or in the company we keep, we will never fully turn to God to find value. It is only when all other options, all other rivers -though they look cleaner- finally show themselves as useless, will we ever *fully* turn to God and say, "Yes, Lord. I am ready to go completely in the direction you say."

A few years ago, a friend was telling about an experience which illustrates this point. He was leading a backpacking trip on the Appalachian trail when one of the youth in his group began to have a violent seizure. My friend described it as similar to what one experiences with drug withdrawal. The young boy started shaking, turning pale, moaning, and just basically scaring the pants off the rest of the group. My friend was in a panic. They were out in the middle of nowhere. Even if they could carry the boy the two hours to the road, it would be at least another hour until they reached real medical help. My friend had little, if any, medical training. The extent of his experience had basically been confined to putting Band-Aids on his kid's knees. In his own words, "I was freaking out!"

My friend was out there, in the middle of nowhere, with a kid who, for all practical purposes, was dying right before his eyes. Guess what my friend's emotional state was? Yep! He was desperate! Though he was a very committed Christian up to that point, God had never seen fit to give him the gift of healing or even much of a desire to talk about that aspect of faith. But desperate times deserve desperate measures. There was nothing else my friend could do. There was no human help available. The only hope for the boy was to drag him to his knees and give everything over to God.

That is exactly what they did. They literally drug the boy down on the ground and had a prayer meeting right in the middle of the Appalachian Trail. My friend said, "It was eerie. Almost instantaneously the boy came to himself and was healed."

A coincidence? I don't think so. A miracle? Yes! Most definitely. But here is the point: One of the reasons why we do not regularly know that type of power and usefulness in our lives is because we are rarely in positions where we are flat out of options, desperate, and forced to lean on the Spirit of God.

If you are still skeptical about this, allow me another opportunity to illustrate. I was raised a preacher's kid. My father was a dynamic preacher and minister. He served on the Board of Discipleship for the United Methodist Church in Nashville, Tennessee for three years. During that time, he traveled all over the country and the world sharing the Gospel of Jesus and being an instrument for literally thousands to come to know God. Twice in the Florida conference he was used to take two struggling churches and change them into dynamic tools for the kingdom. When he died at the young age of 53, he was serving a church which had 90 people in attendance his first Sunday and around 2000 his last. There were over 1800 people in attendance at his funeral. He wrote the books *Invite* and *Good Marriages Just Don't Happen* as well as produced a video series based on his marriage book.

I share all of this to say that when I was called into the ministry, it was not the happiest day of my life. First of all, I had seen the countless hours my father spent as a minister.

Contrary to popular belief, most ministers do work a little more than two hours a week. My father was *definitely* one of those. Being aware of this huge drain on his time, I knew I was too lazy to put in the time and commitment of my father, and did not want to live the rest of my life feeling guilty. So, I was not real thrilled with the calling.

Secondly, I was not thrilled about being called into the ministry because I knew I would be following in my father's footsteps. As you could probably surmise, those were some seriously big shoes to fill. I wish there was a better word to use than "intimidated," but right now that is the best word to express how I felt.

Though I was intimidated, I still knew God had called me into the ministry and somewhere in the back of my mind I believed God was going to use me in some significant way. To make a very long story short, I had many ups and some downs in the early years of my ministry. God used my bumbling and stumbling to do some decent ministry in the church I served while in seminary. My first appointment after graduation was two churches in the rural mountains of North Carolina. The best description of the few years there would be a roller coaster. Though having "ups and downs" is not all that unusual for a person's first few years in the ministry, I found myself getting more and more frustrated and disillusioned. To be honest, I expected more out of me. I thought that if I worked hard enough and if I had enough talent, then I could do great ministry. It was not that I left God out of the picture. It had more to do with my belief that I was supposed to have a big part in the picture.

Thank the good Lord, He was able to use my bumbling and stumbling over those five years. What finally got my attention, what ultimately woke me up and made me look deeper into my self, my faith, and the ministry God had called me to was when my father died of a brain tumor and I began to sink into what the Psalmist described as "the valley of the shadow of death."

I was still able to stand up Sunday after Sunday and say what I knew the Bible said. I still talked about Jesus, new life, the Holy Spirit, and the like. My messages did not change.... much. The primary difference was that I was not sure I believed what I was preaching.

I could not even talk about prayer. After thousands had prayed for my father's healing without results, scriptures like, "Ask for whatever you want, in my name, and it will be done for you." (John 14:14) or "Again, I tell you that if two of you on earth agree about anything you ask for, it will be done for you by my Father in heaven." (Matthew 18:19) almost turned my stomach. No, let me put it bluntly. I was convinced scriptures like these were out-right lies. I concluded that these scriptures were put in the Bible probably as an attempt to make God more "marketable." In reality they were just a "bait and switch" technique: God gets you hooked and then He tells you how it's *really* going to be. Obviously, I was in deep despair. The problem with throwing out one part of the Bible is who is to say what is and is not true in the remaining portion? I did not know what I believed.

About the same time of my dark night of the soul, I was preparing for ordination in my denomination.

In order to work toward ordination, the ministerial candidate must serve at least two years in a local church. Near the middle of the second year, the "candidate" must write a set of papers and appear before another group of committees. My papers were being written during this trek through the valley of the shadow of death. Not only that, on the eve of my appointment with the interviewing committees, a close friend of mine called me from the hospital and informed me that he had just tried to commit suicide. All of this was taking place on the anniversary of my father's death. Needless to say, I walked into those committee meetings numb, dumb, and totally ripped apart. To put it bluntly, the committees turned me down flat!!

By "turned me down" most people usually mean they are "deferred". This means the committees will make recommendations concerning areas to work on and allow the candidate to come back the next year and try again. I was turned down by *every* committee. Not only was I turned down, but one very astute and caring person recommended not only psychiatric help -which I would readily admit I needed that day- but that I think about another profession.

I was devastated! Looking back, I completely agree with their decisions. I would have turned me down as well. However, on *that* particular day of rejection, I was not quite as objective.

On my way home, I cried, I screamed, I yelled, and I pounded the dashboard. I wish I could climb into the minds of those people who drove past and saw me having a "conniption". I am sure a few of them called the cops. It was not a pretty sight. I had let God, myself, my family, and my father down. I was embarrassed and humiliated. Guess what word best describes the state I was really in. Can you think of it? The word is **Broken**.

Without any question in my mind, *that* day was the beginning of the end of one type of minister. Before that date, always in the back of my mind were the thoughts:
"I wonder how this looks."
"Will this make me *successful*."
"What will others think of me."
After that day, all the other options started to fade away like dying weeds, leaving only one life-giving Vine.

After I had settled down in my truck on the way home, I heard God plainly saying to me, "Jim, if you are going to be *My* apostle, then you are going to have to be *MY* apostle. *I* have to call the shots. *I* have to direct the path. It is *MY* Spirit you must rely on. I am not making any promises except that with Me, *fully Mine*, you will be where you need to be. Trust Me."

I did. In that moment, I handed Jim Martin over to the Lord. It no longer mattered to me where I served, who I was, what people thought, or if I had a "career" or not. What mattered was: **AM I HIS**?

Did this new surrender mean that everything in my ministry had been useless up to that point. No. Surprisingly, I have been told by a number of people who suffered under my ministry in the years prior to that event that God had used me to work in their lives. I guess Spurgeon was right, "God *can* use our bumbling everything better than our perfect nothing." In other words, God can use what we make available to Him, even if it is tainted, scared, and restricted.

BUT...... Are you paying attention? God can do a whole lot more, *and* we can have a lot more fun in the "doing," with a life that is totally His. What made the difference? What brought me to a huge growth point in my walk with God? I was broken.

Have you ever been broken? Do you truly want to know the peace, power, joy, comfort, love, and acceptance of walking with God in a fully surrendered way? Maybe the first step is to pray that you would be brought low; that all of your options, all but The Option, be taken away. When that happens, look for God.

CHAPTER 28
Say Please

"Which of you fathers, if your son asks for a fish, will give him a snake instead? Or if he asks for an egg, will give him a scorpion? If you then, though you are evil, know how to give good gifts to your children, how much more will your Father in heaven give the Holy Spirit to those who ask him!"
(Luke 11:11-13 NIV)

Of all the complaints I hear from married couples about one another, the biggest is: "He/She expects me to read his/her mind!" The remarks go something like this: The wife will say, "He never says 'I love you!' He never does anything which, without a doubt, tells me that he loves me. His excuse is always: 'But look at what I do for you. You should *know* I love you.' Sometimes I just need to hear him say it."

The husband will almost always say something like: "She is always wanting me to read her mind. I'll ask her where she wants to go out to eat for our anniversary. She'll say, 'Anywhere is fine.' I will think to myself, 'Great!' and we'll go to Hardees or a steak joint. We'll have what I *thought* was a good time, until the ride home. She doesn't say a word to me. I'll ask her what's wrong and she'll say, 'You should know.' I should know *what*?! After a little more prodding and pleading, she'll turn to me, with tears in her eyes and say, 'I can't believe you took me to a fast food restaurant on our anniversary. You must not love me anymore!' My jaw will hang open for the one hundredth time that week and I'll say, 'But you said, and I quote, 'Anywhere is fine.' Why say that if you don't mean it. Then she'll say, 'You should have known what I meant. After all of these years together, you should know exactly what I want and how I feel. See, you really don't love me!'"

Sound familiar? It should.

Let me clarify something here: This conversation is completely based on what I have heard others tell me. This situation has never occurred in my house.

The reason I bring up this topic of marital bliss is to point out that this tendency to want our minds and hearts read without any effort to truly express ourselves causes its problems not only in marriages, but regularly rears its ugly head in the area of our relationship with God as well. We believe that if God is truly omnipotent, all knowing, and can read the thoughts and needs of our hearts, why should we bother exerting ourselves in order to make a specific request of Him.

There is *some* validity to that thought. However, if you are thinking that thought, hold it in the back of your mind for a second. There are two things I want to point out in regards to this whole "making our request known to God" idea.

First of all, God constantly tells us in His Word to ask. Secondly, if you think about it, there are some very logical reasons why it is good for our relationship with God to ask.

Let's look first at the concrete instances where God tells us in His Word to ask. Go back and re-read the opening scripture of this section. It does not end with, "God will dump His Holy Spirit on you whether you like it or not." It does not say that if you do certain deeds the Holy Spirit will automatically fall. Jesus clearly says that the Holy Spirit will be given to those who "*ask*."

In both Matthew 7:7 and Luke 11:9, the Gospel writers quote Jesus as saying: "*Ask* and it will be given to you; *seek* and you will find; *knock* and the door will be opened to you." The obvious implication here is that God is waiting to bless those who take the time to ask. Matthew also quotes Jesus saying, "Again, I tell you that if two of you on earth agree about anything you ask for, it will be done for you by my Father in heaven." (Matthew 18:19 NIV) John gets in the game and quotes Jesus saying, "And I will do whatever you ask in my name, so that the Son may bring glory to the Father."

(John 14:13 NIV) Paul writes to the church at Phillipi: "Do not be anxious about anything, but in everything, by prayer and petition, with thanksgiving, present your requests to God." (Phillipians 4:6 NIV) Paul writes to the church at Ephesus: "And pray in the Spirit on all occasions with all kinds of prayers and requests." (Ephesians 6:18 NIV) Finally, James wrote, "If any of you lacks wisdom, he should ask God, who gives generously to all without finding fault, and it will be given to him." (James 1:5 NIV)

This, of course, is just a sampling of the myriad of scriptures encouraging us to ask. Even if God does know our requests before we make them, (Matthew 6:8), we are still constantly told to ask. The next question would be, "What *are* the logical reasons behind God desiring that we make specific requests of Him?"

Learn to Speak

One of the first reasons is illustrated by a story I heard from my father back in my junior high years. He told of a family he had worked with early in his ministry. Two very distraught parents came into his office and asked for help. The problem was that their child, now four years old, had not yet begun to talk. The child would cry and periodically mumble something close to "mommy" or "daddy," but had made little if any progress in being able to communicate. My father sat quietly and listened to their struggles, worries, and pain. After a little while, he asked them if they had seen a professional about their child's problem. They answered, "Oh no! We wanted someone objective to look at the seriousness of the problem before we sought professional help."

My father talked with them a few minutes longer and then rescheduled a time to get together at their house where he would have a better opportunity to watch their son in his natural habitat. They thanked him for his help, and went home with at least a glimmer of hope in their hearts.

About a week later, my father showed up at the scheduled time, went into the kitchen with the family, and under the guise of a regular ministerial visit, watched the child. What he saw floored him. Right in the middle of his conversation with the parents, the child walked into the kitchen, pointed in the direction of the refrigerator, the cabinet, or whatever he wanted and said, "UH!" In response to the boy's grunt, either the mother or the father would immediately jump up and wait on his every need. After a few more interruptions like this, one of the older siblings came into the house and jumped into the same act. If the mute child pointed in the direction of the toy box, the sibling would start taking out toys until the child smiled. If the child smacked his lips as if they were dry, one of the other siblings would quickly get up and go get the child something to drink.

As my father watched all of this, he did everything he could to keep himself from laughing. He knew the parents were very concerned and embarrassed about their child's problem, and probably would not be overly thrilled that the minister was getting such a kick out of their predicament. Dad walked into the next room, patted the young boy on his head, and motioned for the parents to follow him outside. Once there, he gave them this suggestion: "Don't cater to your child's every need. More than that, make him ask for what he wants. This is just a guess, but from what I see, there has been no need for your son to learn to talk. Everybody in the house seems to be ready, willing, and able to read his mind. He may pitch a fit. It may take a few weeks. But if you give it a try, you may discover that he is able to talk, and just has not had a reason to do it."

With that earth-moving advice, he left them to deal with a kid who was in for the shock of his life.

A few weeks later these same parents came running into my dad's office with big smiles on their faces. They enthusiastically shook his hand and said, "It worked! It was tough there for the first week or so. He screamed and fussed like a mad man. But you were right. Once we stopped reading his mind and doing everything for him, he began to speak just like any other child."

They paused, and then looked at each other with knowing smiles, turned back to my father and asked, "Now. How do we shut him up?" They all had a good laugh, shared a hug or two, and left with real gratitude and hope in their hearts.

What is the point? Simply this: Just as little children grow and develop through the necessity of asking, so do babes in Christ begin to grow up and learn to articulate their faith through the process of "making their requests known to God." To put it quite bluntly, God apparently wants us to ask so that we will not grow up to be spoiled, rotten brats expecting Him to fulfill our every whim.

Acknowledge our need for God

Asking acknowledges our oun insufficiency and our need for God. In other words, our *asking* for God to fill us with His Spirit and immerse us in His presence is a clear witness that we have been broken and that we do recognize that we are incomplete without Him. In this situation, the asking is not as much a part of the process as it is a testimony to the reality of what has come before: Getting ready for the filling.

I will again use my father as an example. I have always had a fascination with wood. From the time I was a little kid, I liked to get scraps of wood and nail them together into some sort of recognizable shape. Though they never resembled what I intended them to resemble, the results were always, shall we say, "interesting." To tell you the truth, I am convinced that modern art was the result of some out of work sculptor finding one of my "earlier pieces" in a dumpster somewhere.

I clearly remember the first time my father let me work with electric saws. My goal was to build a birdhouse. Of course, my mother was a tad concerned about my cutting a leg or a major artery. My father put her mind at ease when he assured her that he had taken precautions to disassemble the big table saw, hide the circular saw, and leave me with only the jigsaw. For those of you who are not in the know about wood working tools, a "jigsaw" is nothing more than an electric hand saw. About the only thing you can cut quickly with it is butter. One may be able to cut the skin, but loosing major limbs was really not in the cards.

There I was, out in the garage, cutting, banging, nailing, measuring. Generally in that order, too. I would cut here, nail there, only to find that I forgot to measure first. Needless to say, my bird house was taking on the familiar modern art sculpture appearance of my previous works. Though I heed his advice now, back then I totally ignored it when my father said, "Always remember: measure twice, cut once."

I must have worked on that birdhouse for days. I would come home from school, do my homework and chores, and then sprint out to the garage to complete my creation. Periodically, my father would stand and peek out the window of the door to see how I was doing. The strange thing about him watching me was that even when I was messing up, getting frustrated, and on the verge of throwing the whole thing in the trash for some unemployed artist to find, my dad never came out and offered his help. I would find myself biting my tongue, just on the verge of speaking in strange languages to my birdhouse, and glance over to the door just in time to see my father duck away. I wondered then if maybe my father was some type of sadistic freak or someone who got his jollies out of watching his children suffer. Finally! After three or four days of frustration and little progress, I walked into the house, and "plopped down" in front of my father -clearly communicating my frustration. After a few minutes given for dramatic effect, I asked, "Dad, will you come out and help me. I just can't seem to get it."

He said, "Sure!" then hopped up and followed me outside to my project.

Was there an ulterior motive to my father's lack of helping. You bet there was! He wanted me to learn how to try again, on my own. But I discovered *the* ulterior motive when we walked out of the house and picked up the project. He paused with it for a minute and said, "Son, don't ever be ashamed to ask for help. It doesn't mean you failed. It just means you need something else to help you succeed."

Communion

Asking is a part of communing.

"Making our requests known to God" is a vital part of our communicating, relating, and being in touch with the presence of God. If God answered our prayers before we ever allowed them to move from our inner spirit, through our minds, and into our mouths, we would lose much of the hands on feel of being in relationship with God.

A friend of mine told me about a fishing trip he took years ago with his boss. He said that for years his boss had gotten together with some old buddies to do a little deep sea fishing at the coast. Every year it was the same bunch of guys gathering together at the same place, telling the same old jokes and stories. After so many years, and no one having any new stories to tell, they had gotten tired of retelling the same old jokes and stories, so they gave each joke and story a number. My friend said that it took him awhile to catch on to what was happening.

The first night after fishing, they were all sitting around playing cards, when one of the old timers called out, "ONE!" There was a brief pause, followed by side splitting laughter. After a few minutes, one of the other guys asked, "Do y'all remember Four?" Almost in unison they responded, "Oh yeah! That was a good one!" and started to laugh again. Needless to say, my friend was a little lost. After they explained the whole process to him, he had a good chuckle about the situation, but still was never quite able to get into the flow.

Take that same situation and move it over to marriage. Let's say a couple has been together so long that they know every move, blink, and signal. In fact, they have worked out cute little codes between themselves to say anything from, "This party is boring. Get sick so we can leave." to "I love you." At first, most of us would agree that it takes a special degree of closeness to have your own unspoken language. But think about the results of that on a long term basis. How long will a little wink fill in for a loving touch or a cuddle on the couch? How long will a touch of the ear which says, "I really don't want to talk about this," last in lieu of some real quality heart to heart conversations. Not long. Though the signals may remain, the relationship will eventually grow cold and meaningless. Sooner or later, so too will the signals.

The same is true of God. Though there are wonderfully special times in our relationship where just a nod or a brief wink communicates to God what is on our hearts, if we do *only* that, in lieu of real communion and communication, soon the relationship will grow cold and even our little signals will lose their meaning.

We need to ask in order to deepen the communion between us and God.

A Part of the Process

We need to ask because asking makes *us* a part of the process. Consider the difference between someone saying, "I really need to stop smoking," and "Will you help me to stop smoking?" The first statement truthfully delays our having to deal with our need to stop smoking. Anytime someone says, "I really need to....." and then declares some vice, they are in essence saying, "I really need to do this, but I have no real intentions of doing this. I just wanted to let *you* know that I know so that you won't bug me about it for awhile."

On the other hand, "Will you help me to stop smoking?" is a commitment. Anytime we ask anyone to be a part of what we are doing, we are encouraging another party to keep tabs on our progress. Once we have asked another party to keep tabs on our progress, we are more likely to work toward *making* progress.

If we ask God to help us get out of the picture, we are basically committing to do all that *we* can to be a part of that process.

SO..... "Ask and it will be given unto you."

CHAPTER 29
Listen for the Tick

*"On one occasion, while he (Jesus) was eating with them, he gave them this command: 'Do not leave Jerusalem, but **wait** for the gift my Father promised, which you heard me speak about.'" (Acts 1:4 NIV)*

"**Y**ou will have to *wait!*" The words grate on our nerves almost as badly as a dentist's drill. "You will have to" are not the words which necessarily bother us. If someone were to say, "You will have to take this million dollars whether you like it or not," we probably would not be terribly upset. If a young lady heard, "You will have to marry this wonderful guy because he loves you," I am sure it would make her day. Though "You will have to" does tend to be a little restrictive, the word that really gets under the skin -especially of modern day Americans- is "WAIT"!

We hear it all the time. We rush to the market, run like an Indianapolis driver through the isles, throwing our goods in the basket, and hurry up to the register, only to find that the line stretches all the way through the store to the dried fruit section. We are disgusted that we have to wait. Even if there is only ONE person ahead of us, the fact that we are delayed only a few minutes starts many of us ranting and raving about never patronizing that particular store again.

Have you ever called a company and the person answers the phone with, "Will you hold please?" and puts you on hold before you even have a chance to say "Yes" or "No"? Just once I would like to have the nerve to say when they finally come back on the line, "Oh, by the way, since you did not even have the courtesy to let me respond, I did not get a chance to tell you that you had 10 seconds to win one million

232

dollars if you could tell me the first president of the United States. Nine, Ten! Oh well. Too late. Better luck next time!"

We hate to wait!

Not only do we hate to wait for things that we have limited control over, like doctor's offices, help lines, service at restaurants, etc., we especially dislike waiting for things which we *do* have some control over. As stated earlier, when I first went into the ministry, I had visions of being "successful." Back then "successful" meant having a large number of people coming to my church. Since large numbers is a measurable and obtainable goal, I set out with great enthusiasm to do anything and everything it took to bring in those numbers. If I heard that there was a program which promised instant "evangelistic" growth, I would get my hands on the material as fast as possible and implement it with lightening speed. Without exception, in every instance, because I went off half cocked without any leading from God, the "bullet" never reached its target, and there I would sit, wondering why the people would not come. By the grace of God, there was some response, but what I generally ended up with were both a tired minister and bewildered congregation.

But even the lack of numerical success did not stop me. I decided that if success could not be measured -since I could not obtain it- by numerical means, then it must be measured by how busy I stayed and how much time I expended on any given program or projects. The idea of waiting for God to move, was one of the furthest things from my mind. I had places to go, things to do, people to overwhelm. Like a female gymnast, I had only so many years of productive ministry and then I was going to be put out to pasture. I had to get the work done while the getting was good. Wait for God to move? Not on your life!

Yet, one of *the* direct instructions Jesus gave to his disciples was to wait: "Do not leave Jerusalem, but **wait**...." Why? If God sent Jesus to save the world, why would the Disciples have to wait? I would think God would give them the Spirit right then and there, and get the show on the road. Why wait?

Why should we wait? If it is God's desire and goal for us to become immersed in His presence and out of the picture, why wait? Why not simply fill us up immediately and let us get on with the joy of being complete?

Timing

If for no other reason, we should wait because there is a proper time and place for everything. The writer of Ecclesiastes had it right when he said that there is a time for everything.... a time to be born and a time to die, a time to plant and a time to uproot. There, too, is a time when we are more receptive to that total infilling of God. A part of that receptivity has to do with being broken and realizing the significance of what it means to be immersed in the Spirit of God.

We need to be ready and willing to wait for the time God knows is best.

Receive Fully

I have found that we need to wait in order to *fully* receive what God has in store for us.

The disciples in the Acts account are a perfect example. If they had been given the declaration, "Go into all the world and make disciples" and had immediately started preaching based on their *own* power, authority, and understanding, they would have flopped big time! It would have been a disaster. It would have been a disaster much like my experiences with running off half-cocked on my own enthusiasm with every program which came down the pike. The disciples had to wait until the proper time for them to receive, *and* the proper time for them to stand and boldly proclaim the Gospel. Remember, it was because of the Jewish celebration of Pentecost that there were thousands of people to hear Peter's first message. What had happened if the disciples had been filled, and had run out into empty streets to proclaim the Good News of Jesus? Probably next to nothing!

Heart Conditioning

Another part of our waiting and being ready has to do with the conditioning of our own heart. It seems we appreciate things more when they have not been flippantly and instantly given to us.

Wait. It is necessary. It is hard. It is what Jesus said must be. But our narrow understanding of the word "wait" does not quite complete the image of what it takes for us to get out of the picture. Though "wait" covers some aspects of how immersion becomes a reality in our lives, **"Be still"** fulfills it. The writer of the forty-sixth Psalm wrote: "Be still and know that I am God." (Psalm 46:10 NIV) What did he mean by that? Exactly what it says: Only when we intentionally slow down and quiet our lives can we make ourselves available for God to pour Himself into us.

Have you ever been on a merry-go-round at a playground? Have you ever been a kid on one of those merry-go-rounds and your dad is spinning you around so fast you think you are going to "horkle" a lung? I've been there. It is not a pretty sight. I remember camping with my family at a state park in Georgia when I was around six years old. My father took us to the playground, and after considerable begging, started pushing my brother and me on the merry-go-round. I remember him saying, "Try and keep your eyes on me. I bet you can't do it!"

The first couple of rounds we could. No problem. But after awhile, I could not keep my eyes on anything. Finally, I yelled, "Stop! I'm going to be sick!" As every good father should, he spun me around a few more times and then stopped. I fell off the "equipment of death," wobbled over to a grassy area and collapsed. Here is a quiz question: What did I need to do in order to be able stand again, see clearly, and walk with my father? I would need to lay there and *be still.*

Think of pouring life-giving water from a pitcher into a smaller glass. If we are the glass and God is the pitcher, how well do you think that pouring process is going to go if the glass keeps jumping and running all over the place? Not very well! In fact, if a few drops make it into the glass, it would be a surprise. We need to learn to be still.

When I take a group backpacking on the Appalachian Trail, almost everything we eat is prepared with hot water. Almost everything we eat is instant. The hikers put their instant.... whatever in their cups, come to us for the hot water, and we pour it in. The problem comes when those who are receiving the water try to assist us in the pouring. As I am holding a scalding hot pot with my ever-warming pot holder, I take aim at their little back-packing cups so as not to pour boiling water on an exposed hand. As I am taking aim, invariably the person holding the cup will raise it to the spout of the pot. Every time they raise it, I have to lift it higher in order to keep the water from going down their arm. Eventually, I wind up hanging from a tree in order to pour the water into the ever-moving cup. When the next person comes up, the whole process starts over again. Finally, I become frustrated enough to say -in a very gentle and loving manner- "Hold the cup still. I'll do the pouring. You just do the receiving." Sometimes the very reason we are not being immersed in the presence of God is that we refuse to get off the merry-go-round of life and slow down; *or* we are trying too hard. Sometimes what we need is to simply be still, and then God can pour Himself into us and not spill a drop.

Probably the best illustration of how we need to wait and be still in order to know the Lord, is a story, I heard years ago from another preacher.

The story begins with a grandfather losing a very expensive and precious gold watch. He was visiting with his daughter's family and had gotten out of his routine of placing the watch in a specific place. As anyone would expect, he began to panic a little at the prospect of never finding the watch again. In his effort to find the watch, he almost tore the house apart. He carried out his search exactly how I searched for my keys that hot Georgia afternoon. He started with the "first run through," moved quickly to the "meticulous search" mode, and arrived at the "grab and slam" with gusto and vigor. All the time the grandfather searched, his grandson watched. After the grandfather had exhausted himself, as well as all the technically correct search modes, he collapsed onto his bed and sat there panting.

After a few minutes, his grandson walked up and said, "Granddad, I have an idea. Why don't we just sit in some room quietly and listen. Maybe we'll be able to hear the watch."

That was just what they did. After a few minutes, when the house noises had eased, and the heavy breathing of the grandfather had subsided, the boy began to hear a faint but distant tick. He got up immediately, but the minute he started to move, he lost the sound. So, he stood where he was, silently, and listened. Again he heard the tick. He took a few steps in that direction and stopped. He stopped just long enough to hear the tick and then moved toward it again. This process continued until, finally, the boy was standing in front of the dresser and hearing the watch loud and clear. He moved the dresser, and there, to his grandfather's joy, was the watch. They had found the watch!

Or did the watch find them?

And the words of the Psalmist come ringing through loud and clear: "Be still and know that I am God."

Silently the green leaves grow,
In silence falls the soft, white snow.
Silently, the flowers bloom
In silence sunshine fills a room.
Silently bright stars appear
In Silence velvet night draws near...
And silently God enters in
To free a troubled heart from sin

For God works silently in lives
For nothing spiritual survives
Amid the din of noisy street
Where raucous crowds with hurrying feet
And "blinded eyes" and "deafened ear"
Are never privileged to hear
The message God wants to impart
To every troubled, weary heart
For only in a quiet place
Can man behold God face to face. (Author unknown)

CHAPTER 30

Take The Step

"Instead of their shame my people will receive a double portion, and instead of disgrace they will rejoice in their inheritance; and so they will inherit a double portion in their land, and everlasting joy will be theirs." (Isaiah 61:7 NIV)

My children have never been really big on trying new things. Like their father, they tend to get into a comfortable and safe rut and stay there. To this day, my wife gives me a hard time about eating the same thing for breakfast and lunch almost every day of the year. I guess I should not be too surprised that my two girls are not real fans of trying different foods.

When my youngest was about four years old, we were getting the table set for the typical American Thanksgiving dinner. Thanksgiving is one of those days when I do eat something other than my boring sandwich and chips. One of the "delicacies" of the Martin Thanksgiving dinner is black olives. For as long as I can remember, we have had black olives at our house for Thanksgiving and Christmas. For years, I thought that they must be terribly expensive and hard to come by due to their rare appearance on our table. So, I relished every morsel. Since they were so special to me, I wanted to pass on the value of this delicacy to my kids.

I failed miserably to help my oldest daughter acquire a taste. Actually, it was my wife's fault. A few years before, when I suggested my oldest daughter try some, my wife said, "EWWW! How can you eat those things. She's not going to like them. They'll make her puke and die."

Truthfully, my wife was not that dramatic. That quote, however, is not far from what she *did* say. Needless to say, my oldest daughter refused to eat what was going to make her puke and die. Even today, she would rather be rolled in honey and placed on an ant hill than eat black olives.

My last chance for keeping alive the family legacy of eating black olives was in my youngest daughter. As we were placing the food on the plates, I picked up a few black olives and strategically placed them next to the green beans on her plate in hopes that she would not notice and accidentally eat one or two. Alas, ever aware of her surroundings, she saw my sly move and grabbed the plate from my hands and covered it with her arm. With a face of concern and defiance she said, "What are *THOSE*? I don't want them.!"

Knowing that I had to handle this situation with care and decorum, I very lovingly said, "Honey dear. These are good. I think they are wonderful. They will make you happy and wise all of your life. Besides, they taste good."

She looked over at my wife who had already received the "Don't blow this or I'll kill you look" from me. Her mother just smiled and said, "Go ahead. Try one."

My youngest became suspicious when her older sister started to laugh one of those laughs you hear from mad scientists in the movies just before their victim swallows poison. I said, "Ignore your sister. What does she know? Here, try one."

I motioned to place the lone black olive on her plate when suddenly, there was no more plate. In fact, there was no more daughter. She had taken her plate and had run out of the kitchen. What ensued was a chase rivaled only by a scene from the movie "The French Connection." If we would have had time, we would have gotten the whole episode on video. There I was, a supposedly grown man, chasing my four year old around the house with a lethal vegetable. All the while she's screaming and shouting, enjoying every minute of it.

Finally, I cornered this exhausted and whipped little vegetable hold-out. As we both faced off, panting to beat the band, I said, "Just try one bite and I'll leave you alone."

She looked me over a few times, just to insure that I knew that if I was tricking her, she would leave home and join the circus. She then moved her arm from over the plate and allowed me to put the olive right in the middle where the whole world could see it. She sniffed it. Moved it around with her finger. Gave it a light lick, clinched her eyes, and then took a big bite. After only a few seconds, her face relaxed, her eyes popped open and a smile crept across her lips. She liked it! In fact, she liked them so much that now, at special occasions, we have to get two cans of olives; one for her and one for me. When my brother is eating with us, we get three cans.

What is the point? She may have had her doubts. It may have been something she was not used to and it could possibly change her life, but ultimately, all she needed to do was move her arm and *receive*.

That's it! If what is written in this book is something you would like to have happen in your life; if you want to know the unparalleled life that is available when we begin to get out of the picture, if you would like God to freely pour His Spirit into yours and be immersed in His Presence, then ultimately you have to take your hands off the top of the jar and allow Him to pour. If God is who He says He is, you **will** receive.

I bet once you do receive, you will never put your hand back over the jar again.

"Father, make us willing, empty vessels to be filled with your life giving Spirit. Lord, fill us to the point that when others see us, they see a reflection of You. Immerse us in Youself. Get us out of the picture and so that our lives will give You glory. Amen!"